FROM SUBSISTENCE TO EXCHANGE
AND OTHER ESSAYS

NEW FORUM BOOKS

Robert P. George, Series Editor

A list of titles
in the series appears
at the back of
the book

FROM SUBSISTENCE TO EXCHANGE
AND OTHER ESSAYS

Peter Bauer

With an introduction by Amartya Sen

PRINCETON UNIVERSITY PRESS   PRINCETON, NEW JERSEY

Library of Congress Cataloging-in-Publication Data
Bauer, P. T. (Péter Tamás)
From subsistence to exchange and other essays / Peter Bauer : with
an introduction by Amartya Sen.
p.   cm. — (New forum books)
Includes bibliographical references and index.
ISBN 0-691-00667-9 (cl : alk. paper)
1. Economic development.   2. Commerce.   3. Economics.
I. Title.   II. Series.
HD75.B38   2000
338.9—dc21   99-27680

To Nancy

Contents

Introduction

PETER BAUER is in a class of his own as an outstanding economist. The originality, force, and extensive bearing of his writings have been quite astonishing. He is a real pioneer of modern development economics. He is a profound theorist of the process of change that transforms a subsistence or near-subsistence economy into an exchange economy.

Bauer has investigated in a definitive way the general importance of the incentive to produce and consume, even in the most primitive societies, and—related to that—the roles of relative prices and of the parameters of personal and family behaviour. On more specific issues, he has shown the crucial importance of small-scale trade, the significance of capital formation by farmers and traders (often unrecorded in official statistics), and the positive contributions of cash crops (such as rubber, cocoa, and nuts) in promoting exchange and prosperity. Bauer has drawn attention to and analyzed the far-reaching economic importance of what is now called the "informal sector." He has cogently questioned the standard wisdom on the so-called "population problem" and on the alleged benefits of international aid. He has powerfully disputed the standard explanations of Third World poverty (such as colonialism, or unequal exchange, or an inescapable shortage of capital), and discussed how the poverty of a nation can be perpetuated without any malign intervention by others.

Many of Bauer's claims, while resisted at the time, have become a part of the new "establishment" of ideas. Like the old lady who went to see *Hamlet* and felt it was full of quotations, a young reader of Bauer's early books may find his arguments rather familiar. This is, to a great extent, evidence of his triumph, though the new enthusiasts for Bauer's ideas often do not give him enough credit. He has presented novel and powerful arguments in defence of positions which had been, at that time, quite out of the mainstream. He has been a champion of international trade, even when it used to be viewed with great scepticism by most development theorists (and when even the defenders of international trade seemed to be more engaged in identifying contrary cases than in showing the basic rationale of trade). Now that the mainstream in development economics has caught up with him on international trade, there remain further lessons—not yet fully absorbed—to be learned from his work. The lessons can vary from the pivotal importance of *domestic* trade and the emergence of the *exchange economy*, to the need to see the population problem without ignoring the basic fact that it is the presence and creativity of people that make this inert planet the lively place it is.

Altogether, Bauer has been a consistent and cogent defender of the role of the market economy in bringing about economic development. No one has done more in clarifying the reach of Adam Smith's thesis regarding the creative contributions of exchange. Indeed, Bauer's writings are characterized by systematic use of the basic insights of classical mainstream economics to enhance the understanding of problems that have often been approached without those insights.

Outside economics, his writings have influenced the work of many anthropologists and other social scientists engaged in studying poorer economies and processes of change occurring there. Also, theorists of history have had the opportunity to learn from Bauer's scepticism of the possibility of general theories of history. (John Hicks, a leading twentieth-century economic theorist, acknowledged this in including in the Spanish edition of his own attempt at a theory of history the full text of Bauer's critique of Hicks.) The role of culture in economic development and change is a recurring theme in Bauer's writings. So is his consistent critique of economic egalitarianism as an ideal, disputing its feasibility and identifying the unfavourable consequences for liberty and freedom of a relentless pursuit of equality.

This collection of Bauer's writings will give the reader a fine opportunity to benefit from his wide-ranging intellect and from his powerful use of cogent reasoning in analyzing political economy in general as well as development economics in particular. The book is not, of course, meant as a complete guide to Bauer's life-long work. For that the reader will have to consult, in addition, his earlier books: *The Rubber Industry* (1948), *West African Trade* (1964), *Markets, Market Control and Marketing Reform* (1968), *Dissent on Development* (1971), *Equality, the Third World and Economic Delusion* (1981), *Rhetoric and Reality* (1984), and *The Development Frontier* (1991). But nevertheless, these *Essays in Political Economy* have a wide thematic coverage, giving the reader a taste of many of his major ideas and of their extensive implications.

Peter Bauer's analysis of the role of the market, including domestic as well as international trade, and his pioneering work on the phenomenon of the emergence of an exchange economy receive concentrated presentation in Essay I ("From Subsistence to Exchange"), and also get considerable attention in Essays II ("Disregard of Reality"), VI ("Western Guilt and Third World Poverty"), and X ("Effective Influence on Opinion: The Shenoy Memorial Lecture"). His critique of the common understanding of the "population problem" and his resounding—and reasoned—confidence in the creative potential of people find forceful exposition in Essays III ("The Land and the People") and IV ("Population Explosion: Disaster or Blessing"). The "low down" on foreign aid is delivered—no holds barred—in Essay V ("Foreign Aid: Abiding Issues"). Cultural influences on economic change figure prominently in Essays VII ("The Liberal Death Wish") and VIII ("Ecclesiastical Economics: Envy Legitimized"). Bauer's analysis of class and stratification, and his critique of egalitarianism, can be found in Essays XI ("Class on the Brain") and XII ("Egalitarianism: A Delicate Dilemma").

This selection of essays may not be a comprehensive guide to Bauer's versatile and multifaceted contributions. But it is nevertheless a splendid introduction to some of the main lines of analysis that have been so successfully pursued by Peter Bauer.

A final comment. One does not have to be in full agreement with Bauer to benefit greatly from his works. Even when there is disagreement, Bauer's analysis is always valuable to study and scrutinize. This is one of the things I learned as a student at Cambridge in the 1950s, when I was persuaded by some of his arguments and remained sceptical of others. We met first when he was a very established teacher and I was a young and inexperienced student. He treated me as if we were equal and did his best to set me right—not always with success. But I was forced to examine more critically my own beliefs and arguments. Even when we continued to disagree, I had greatly profited from our encounters. It was important to examine how one might respond to Peter Bauer's persuasive critique. I have been fortunate in having Peter as a friendly challenger throughout my academic life.

Peter Bauer is a major asset not only for those who are on "his side" of the disputes but also to those who disagree with him—mildly or even severely. The dialectical excellence of this selection of essays goes far beyond its value—important as it must be—to his devout followers and to the larger group of people who decide, on balance, to go along with him. Even those who continue to disagree—on this issue or that—must come to terms with the scientific merits of his work. They must reflect critically on the challenges posed by his well-researched findings and his well-reasoned and forceful arguments.

The indispensability of Bauer's analyses is a reflection of the reach and profundity of his political economy. The world of empirical understanding and practical reason that Peter Bauer has created is a robust addition to the discipline of economics in general and to development economics in particular. Even if we choose not to live *within* his world, we cannot live *without* it either. This selection of essays will give the readers a wonderful opportunity to learn about the rich world of cognizance and analysis erected by one of the great architects of political economy. I feel privileged to be able to issue this letter of invitation.

Amartya Sen

FROM SUBSISTENCE TO EXCHANGE
AND OTHER ESSAYS

I

From Subsistence to Exchange

WHEN economists discuss contemporary growth in advanced Western countries, they do not think of internal trade (i.e., wholesale and retail trade) as one of the engines of growth. And they are right. It would be misplaced to associate current economic growth in the West specifically with the distributive sector. Instead, when economists discuss wholesaling and retailing in advanced Western economies, they focus on such subjects as the organization of these activities, the nature and extent of competition, concentration, economies of scale, vertical integration, and restrictive practices. The emphasis is on efficiency in the provision of distributive services: in broad terms, efficiency in the link between production and consumption.

It is unusual to examine the possibility of any relationship between the activities of traders and the growth of the economy, except to the extent that efficiency in the provision of their services releases resources for other purposes. In short, the emphasis is on the allocation of given resources. In this respect, trading activity is treated very much like any other branch of economic activity.

This orientation is justified. It focuses on the main issues of interest to both economists and policymakers. But this orientation, though appropriate now, would be misleading if it were applied to the Western economies as they were two or more centuries ago. Yet in that earlier period those economies were in many ways far more advanced than those of most less developed countries (LDCs) today. In particular, they were already very largely exchange economies in which subsistence or near-subsistence production was relatively unimportant.

INTERNAL TRADE AS AN ENGINE OF GROWTH

Historians have recognized that the economic repercussions of trading activities in, say, seventeenth- and eighteenth-century England went well beyond efficiency in the use of resources in the trading activities themselves.

This paper is a revised and expanded version of the author's lecture presented at the Cato Institute, 14 October 1992, as part of its Distinguished Lecturer Series. Also this paper itself has been expanded for the publication of the present book.

For example, in their book on shopkeeping in eighteenth-century England, Hoh-cheung Mui and Lorna Mui (1989, 291–92) conclude:

> If the major purpose of all these activities by shopkeepers was to drum up business, by so doing they eased the flow of goods and at the same time helped to stimulate as well as satisfy an increasingly widespread demand, a demand that encouraged expansion in industry and overseas trade. It was not an unimportant contributor to the overall economic development of the country—industry, overseas trading and inland distribution moved in tandem, each fructifying the other.

Jacob Price (1989, 283) has observed that in seventeenth- and eighteenth-century Britain the activities of merchants "left behind" much more than "specific markets for specific products." Their activities helped to create commercial institutions and practices and to raise the level of human capital, which proved to be "of great utility to the entire economy in the ensuing era of rapid industrialization and attendant export growth" (p. 283). Richard Grassby (1970, 106) wrote that it was "merchant capital which created markets, financed manufactures, floated the American colonial economies and launched banking and insurance."

In emerging economies the activities of traders promote not only the more efficient deployment of available resources, but also the growth of resources. Trading activities are productive in both static and dynamic senses.[1]

NEGLECT OF TRADING ACTIVITY

One would therefore expect to find that trading activities feature prominently in modern development economics. Instead, in spite of the economic history of the now-developed world, which should have been familiar to development economists, trading activities are barely mentioned in the mainstream literature. It is as if postwar development economics had to begin from scratch, its exponents faced with a tabula rasa.

A charitable interpretation is that exponents of the new development economics thought that early Western experience could not apply to the so-called Third World. This attitude would have been mistaken since it is evident that all developed countries at one time had the characteristics and levels of income and capital of the postwar Third World.

However, even if it were correct to disregard the economic history of the West, the neglect in development economics of the role of trading ac-

---

[1] For a further discussion of the role of traders in the development process, see Bauer (1991, chap. 1).

tivity in the Third World is both unwarranted and surprising. First-hand observation of economic activity in many less developed regions would have shown that trading activity was ubiquitous and that large numbers of people were engaged in it on a full-time, part-time, or casual basis.[2] Moreover, even a cursory reading of the last hundred years' history of some of these regions would have drawn attention to the role of traders in helping to transform them from largely subsistence economies to largely exchange economies. For example, the historian Sir Keith Hancock (1977), after analyzing the major changes in that region, referred to West Africa as the "traders' frontier." Another historian, Allan McPhee, entitled his book, published in London in 1926, *The Economic Revolution in British West Africa*. The book makes clear both that West Africa was transformed in a period of about two generations and also that traders were major agents of that transformation.

The neglect of internal trading activity still persists in mainstream development economics. That this is so is clear from Gerald M. Meier's book *Emerging from Poverty*, published in 1984. Professor Meier is a very distinguished exponent of development economics. His book sets out the main concerns of the subject. Trading activity (as distinct from international trade) is not mentioned.

Had trading activity and its effects been properly appreciated, mainstream development economics would have been radically different. For example, the influential proposition in development economics known as the international demonstration effect portrayed the availability of Western goods as encouraging consumption at the expense of saving and investment, and hence as inhibiting economic growth. However, in reality, trading activity and the availability of imported incentive goods served to initiate and sustain a process in which increases in consumption and investment (for example, in establishing and improving capacity in agriculture) were able to go hand in hand. It is no accident that throughout the Third World the most advanced regions are those with most Western commercial contacts; and, conversely, the most backward and poorest are those with few such contacts. Interestingly, Karl Marx was emphatic in the *Communist Manifesto* about the positive role of cheap consumer goods in the

---

[2] The large numbers involved in trading activities have usually not been reflected in official occupational statistics and official reports. This understatement, or even omission, lends plausibility to the proposition that tertiary activities (which include trading) in poor countries involved a smaller proportion of the labor force than in richer countries and that the proportion increased with economic growth. I examined this proposition, put forward in the 1930s by Colin Clark and Allan G. B. Fisher, in various publications since 1951. There it has been explained why official statistics are misleading and why the empirical and theoretical bases for the Clark-Fisher hypothesis are insubstantial. My views are summarized in my book, *The Development Frontier* (Bauer 1991).

advance from primitive agriculture to more sophisticated and productive economic activity. The concept of incentive goods and the term itself have dropped out of the development literature.

Similarly, the central notion in this literature until quite recently has been the vicious circle of poverty. According to this proposition, poor countries cannot emerge from their poverty because incomes are too low for the saving and investment necessary to raise income. It is difficult to see how development economists could have entertained this notion if they had recognized how millions of poor producers in the Third World had in the aggregate made massive investments in agriculture. These investments were made in the context of their decisions, encouraged by the activities of traders, to replace subsistence production by production for the market. If there had been a vicious circle of poverty, these poor people had failed to notice it. Millions of acres of cultivated land under cash crops such as rubber, cocoa, and coffee, as well as foodstuffs for domestic markets, testify not only to Third World peoples' economic responsiveness and readiness to take a long view but also to the vacuousness of the idea of the vicious circle of poverty.

The notion of the vicious circle of poverty as promoted in the mainstream development literature from the 1940s to at least the 1970s is evidently insubstantial. To have money is the result of economic achievement, not its precondition. That this is so is plain from the very existence of developed countries, all of which originally must have been underdeveloped and yet progressed without external donations. The world was not created in two parts, one with ready-made infrastructure and stock of capital, and the other without such facilities. Moreover, many poor countries progressed rapidly in the hundred years or so before the emergence of modern development economics and the canvassing of the vicious circle. Indeed, if the notion of the vicious circle of poverty were valid, mankind would still be living in the Old Stone Age.

The idea of the vicious circle of poverty has been a major lapse in modern development economics. It has influenced policy considerably. It was a major element in the advocacy of massive state economic controls on the ground that only drastic policies of "resource mobilization" would enable an economy to break the vicious circle. It was also a major strand in the successful advocacy of government-to-government subsidies known as foreign aid.

Lapses in economic thinking are not, of course, confined to modern development economics. One may recall the celebrated near-consensus of economists in the 1950s that the persistent scarcity of the U.S. dollar would be a continuing problem besetting the world economy. This conclusion could be reached only by a now-inexplicable disregard of the rate of exchange (i.e., the price of the dollar). This particular lapse had a short life: the dollar shortage was, in fact, soon replaced by an international glut of dollars. Lapses in modern development economics have proven to be much more impervious to inconvenient evidence. Thus, the notion of the vicious circle of poverty and the disregard of price on quantities supplied and demanded (supply and demand for short), both of which engulfed much mainstream development economics from the late 1940s, persisted for more than two decades. And as I have just noted, disregard of trading has persisted much longer.

One should perhaps say that modern development economics has not neglected traders and trading activity completely. To the very limited extent that these subjects have been considered, the emphasis has been on the so-called imperfections of the market. When not ignored, trade has usually been deplored. Thus, real or alleged monopolistic elements in trade have attracted some attention. For instance, the trader who has penetrated an outlying area is apt to be scrutinized as an individual with market power because he is, after all, the only trader on the spot. The fact that his presence adds to the opportunities available to the local people tends to be ignored.

Winston Churchill, who did not claim economic expertise, saw the point. Writing about East Africa, he said:

> It is the Indian trader who, penetrating and maintaining himself in all sorts of places to which no white man would go or in which no white man could earn a living, has more than anyone else developed the beginning of early trade and opened up the first slender means of communication.[3]

FROM MISFORTUNE TO DISASTER

Market-oriented economists and advocates of extensive state economic control are agreed on one matter, namely that advance from subsistence production to wider exchange is indispensable for a society's escape from extreme poverty. In the absence of opportunities for exchange, there is little scope for the division of labor and the emergence of different crafts or skills. The lack of commercial links with a wider society obstructs or precludes the inflow or emergence of new ideas, methods, crops, and wants. Indeed, unquestioning acceptance of prevailing conditions and the sway of habit and custom are familiar in such economies.

The low level of attainment is accompanied by major hazards. The absence of trading links with the outside world and lack of reserve stocks turn misfortune, such as bad weather, into disaster; belt-tightening becomes starvation. It is not accidental that large-scale famine in the less developed world occurs in subsistence and near-subsistence economies and not in

[3] Quoted in Mangat (1969, 61).

economies already reasonably well integrated into wider regions through exchange relationships. The advance of an economy to wider exchange does not involve greater insecurity as part of the cost of material progress; in other words, there is here no conflict between progress and security.

The misery in Ethiopia, Sudan, and elsewhere in Africa is not the result simply of unfavorable weather, external causes, or population pressure. It is the result of enforced reversion to subsistence conditions under the impact of the breakdown of public security, suppression of private trade, or forced collectivization. There is a core of truth in the jibe that the weather tends to be bad in centrally controlled economies. But although the hazards of a subsistence economy are far more acute than those of an exchange economy, they tend to be politically and psychologically more acceptable as being part of the nature of things and in any case not attributable to human agency. But this greater acceptability of the hazards and hardships of a subsistence economy does not diminish their reality.

Advance from subsistence production involves trading activity. This is obvious at a simple level. There can be no production for sale without an outlet and an accessible conduit to it. Producers also need to buy inputs, such as simple tools and equipment. And they will not produce for sale unless they can use the proceeds to buy goods and services they want. The purchase of inputs and of incentive goods and production for sale are, in turn, closely linked with credit. This is required for the purchase of inputs used in the production of the crops, whether seasonal crops or slow-maturing trees, and also in many cases for sustaining producers until their crops are harvested. Traders are an effective and convenient source and channel of such finance. In these circumstances, production of cash crops, trade, and credit are intertwined.

But the significance of trade extends far beyond these pipeline services. Contacts through traders and trade are prime agents in the spread of new ideas, modes of behavior, and methods of production. External commercial contacts often first suggest the very possibility of change, including economic improvement.

SMALL-SCALE OPERATIONS

Conditions in the Third World tend to ensure the need for a substantial volume of trading and closely related activities. These activities are more labor intensive than in the West because capital is scarcer relative to labor in poor countries than in rich.

A large proportion of producers and consumers operate on a small scale and far from the major commercial centers, including the ports. Individual transactions are small. Individual farmers produce on a small scale and sell in even smaller quantities at frequent intervals because they lack storage facilities and substantial cash reserves. Conversely, because of their low incomes, consumers find it convenient or necessary to buy in small, often very small, amounts, again at frequent intervals. In these conditions the collection of produce and the physical distribution of consumer goods and of farm inputs are necessarily expensive in real terms. Storage, assembly, bulking, transport, breaking of bulk, and distribution absorb a significant proportion of available resources.

In Nigeria, for example, individual groundnut farmers may sell a few pounds of groundnuts at a time and operate 500 to 700 miles from the ports whence the groundnuts are shipped in consignments of thousands of tons. Imported consumer goods arrive in large consignments and are often bought in minute quantities. In Nigeria, matches arrive in consignments of several hundred cases, each case containing hundreds or thousands of boxes. The ultimate consumer may buy only part of a box. The sale of one box is at times a wholesale transaction; the buyer resells the contents in little bundles of ten matches, together with part of the striking surface of a box. Cheap imported scent arrives in large consignments: the ultimate consumer often does not buy even a small bottle but only two or three drops at a time, perhaps a dab on each shoulder of the garment. In some African countries smokers buy single cigarettes, or even a single inhaled drag of a cigarette.

To a Western audience it may seem as if sales of produce and purchases of consumer goods in such small quantities must be wasteful. This is not so. If consumers could not buy in these small quantities, they would either have to tie up their very limited capital in larger purchases or, more likely, would not be able to consume the products at all.[4] The same considerations apply to a farmer's sales of produce to an intermediary.

It is evident that in these conditions the task of collecting and bulking produce and of breaking bulk and physical distribution of merchandise involves much labor. What may be somewhat surprising is that a large part of this labor is self-employed. This is so because entry into small-scale trading is easy. In the absence of officially imposed obstacles such as restrictive licensing or official monopsonies, there are few if any institutional barriers, few administrative skills are needed, and little initial capital is required. The supply price of self-employed labor is low in the absence of more profitable opportunities. For these reasons small-scale operations are economic in many parts of the distribution system: large firms are at a disadvantage because their operations require more administrative and supervisory per-

---

[4] As Adam Smith observed, "Unless a capital was employed in breaking and dividing certain portions either of the crude or manufactured produce, into such small parcels as suit the occasional demands of those who want them, every man would be obliged to purchase a greater quantity of the goods he wanted, than his immediate occasions required." *Wealth of Nations,* Book II, chap. 5.

sonnel, and these tend to be relatively expensive or ineffective in many poor countries. A multiplicity of small-scale traders in part represents the substitution of cheaper labor for more expensive labor.[5]

A colorful illustration of labor-intensive trade is provided by the extensive business in used containers. Petty traders purchase, collect, store, clean, repair, and resell containers such as tins, boxes, bottles, and sacks. They thereby extend the effective life and use of these products. Labor is used, and capital is conserved.

The small-scale trader often does not supply simply marketing services to his customers. In many cases he provides credit, usually in modest sums. This credit is used for such purposes as the purchase of seeds, fertilizers, pesticides, building materials, implements, and consumer goods. The advancing of this credit generally is the final stage in a flow of funds emanating from financial institutions and large trading firms that have direct access to international financial markets. These enterprises advance credit to the larger indigenous traders, the latter advance credit to smaller traders, and so on until the farmer gets his loan. There is, in short, a process of bulk-breaking in the financial market; and the farmer in the hinterland has access indirectly to the world capital market.

A Western audience may be surprised at the relatively large number of successive independent trading intermediaries who typically are involved in the movement of a farmer's output from the first collection to the final shipment from the port. Again, this succession of intermediaries may seem wasteful and suggest that it would be more economic for the flow of goods to pass through fewer successive intermediaries. But this opinion overlooks two considerations already noted: first, the supply price of the services of small traders is very low, and second, a larger vertically integrated trading firm spanning several successive stages would require relatively expensive personnel for coordination and supervision. In the circumstances, the vertical subdivision of trading activities among successive intermediaries is economic. That this is so is ensured by the option to by-pass a redundant intermediary. No producer, consumer, or intermediary is forced to use the services of any intermediary if he can perform that intermediary's services at lower cost: a redundant bulking or bulk-breaking intermediary will be sidestepped. The same is true of any other trading service such as the provision of credit.

It may be helpful if I anticipate a doubt in some readers' minds. It is often contended that farmers in poor countries are not free to choose among intermediaries in selling their produce because they are indebted to

[5] The numbers attracted to trade in LDCs may be increased as a result of rigidities in money wages for hired labor. It was Simon Rottenberg (1953) who first pointed out this necessary qualification. But even if these wages were at market-clearing levels, the numbers who would find trading attractive would still be very large as long as the underlying economic factors remain the same.

particular traders to whom they have to sell their output at a depressed price. However, where the producer can choose among a number of would-be lenders and trader-lenders, he will choose to borrow where the terms are most advantageous to him. The terms of loans from trader-lenders are a combination of interest payments and the obligation to sell the produce to the lender; what in isolation may seem to be a forced sale at a low price may simply represent an indirect part of interest on the loan. And, of course, many producers are not in debt.

In much of the less developed world, especially in Africa, there is no clear-cut distinction between farmers and traders or moneylenders. The small trader is often the more enterprising farmer who collects produce from neighbors or relatives and takes it to the market. After a while, he may come to trade more nearly full time. And even without such progression, the trader or moneylender in rural areas in LDCs, conspicuously so in Africa, is usually very much anchored in the rural community with farming relatives.

In the same way as many Third World farmers have become part-time or full-time traders, so many traders have become manufacturers. Successful traders accumulate capital and develop business skills that are helpful for the conduct of industrial operations. In the words of Adam Smith, "The habits besides of order, economy and attention to which mercantile business naturally forms a merchant render him much fitter to execute, with profit and success any project of improvement" (*Wealth of Nations,* Book III, chap. 4). Throughout the Third World many viable industrial enterprises have been pioneered and developed by traders.

NONMONETARY INVESTMENT

Farmers in poor countries producing for wider exchange have to make investments of various kinds. These investments include the clearing and improvement of land and the acquisition of livestock and equipment. Such investments constitute capital formation. A part of this capital formation is financed from personal savings and borrowing from traders and others. But much of it is nonmonetized. For example, the clearing or improvement of land is the result of additional effort on the part of the farmer and his family. Very little monetary expenditure is involved.

These forms of investment, when made by small farmers, are generally omitted from official statistics and are still largely ignored in both the academic and the official development literature.

In many poor countries these overlooked categories of investment are in the aggregate highly important both quantitatively and qualitatively. They are quantitatively significant because agriculture and the activities closely related to it account for much of economic activity. They are qualitatively significant because these categories of investment are critical in the advance from subsistence to exchange. Moreover, such investments are especially likely to be productive because they are made by people who have a direct interest in the returns.

Besides presenting a misleading picture of economic activity in the Third World, the neglect of this capital formation has had adverse practical consequences. Taxation and other policies have often retarded the expansion of the exchange sector by reducing the farmer's proceeds or by increasing his costs. I believe that these policies would not have been pursued so extensively and intensively if the scale and significance of capital formation on small farms had been recognized.

The reasons for this neglect are necessarily conjectural. But their consequences are clear. This neglect issues in a highly misleading picture of economic activity and of the attitudes of peoples over a large part of the Third World. For instance, in discussions of the plantation rubber industry attention had focused almost entirely on the estate side of the industry to the neglect of the small holdings. Yet in the aggregate this latter category in area and output was at least equal to that of the estates. Cultivated agricultural properties are income-yielding assets, the productivity of which exceeds that of unimproved land as a result of effort and activity. The process of establishing, extending, and improving the land is investment. To disregard it neglects all direct agricultural investment in the nonmonetary sector of the economy and also much of it in the monetary sector when the land is used for the production of cash crops. The disregard of these categories of investment has encouraged the notion that the peoples of the Third World suffer from economic myopia and give no thought for the morrow. It has also lent superficial plausibility to doomsday prophesies of population growth. The neglect of direct agricultural investment also precludes the framing of policy designed to maximize productive saving and investment.

Disregard of this capital formation resembles neglect of the extent and role of trading activity. In both cases the extent and importance of the neglected activity should have been evident from direct observation of economic activity in poor countries. Indeed, reflection on readily available statistics alone would have indicated the importance both of capital formation in agriculture and also of trading activity: statistics such as those regarding exports and imports and the volume of freight handled on the railways, and also changes in those statistics over time, all of which are relevant and informative in this context.

THE SCOPE AND EFFECTIVENESS OF ECONOMICS

I have here been criticizing features of mainstream development economics. Let me recapitulate briefly. In recent decades, major shortcomings disfigured this branch or subdiscipline of economics. These have included the disregard of trading activity; the neglect of major determinants of economic performance such as cultural and political factors; the notion of the vicious circle of poverty; and the practice of price-less economics, that is, the disregard of the relationship between price and quantities supplied and demanded.

These are failures of observation or failures to apply basic economic reasoning. These defects have had serious practical consequences, some of which I have alluded to earlier in this lecture. The neglect of cultural and political factors necessarily involves disregard of the reciprocal interaction between the familiar variables of economic analysis and these determinants of economic performance and progress.

You will appreciate that I am not saying here that economists have little or nothing to contribute by way of explaining economic phenomena and processes in the Third World and thereby assisting in the framing of economic policies. On the contrary, they have much to offer. Economic analysis is generally applicable as a major step in understanding the likely effects of a change in any of the familiar economic variables. Economists working in unfamiliar settings will, however, be more effective if, in addition, they recognize that cultural and political factors, usually taken as given, may be influenced by changes in one or another of these variables. For example, a change in the foreign trade regime, and hence in the availability of imported goods, is likely to affect the spread of new ideas and information and thereby people's attitudes and modes of behavior.

The potentialities of economics both for explanation and policy in poor countries have been enriched by recent advances in other fields of economic enquiry, such as the economic theory of politics and bureaucracies, the economics of property rights, the analysis of the dichotomy between insiders and outsiders in the labor market, the economics of transaction costs, and the theory of effective protection.

Critical assessment of contemporary development economics, therefore, must not serve to obscure the relevance of economics for the understanding of economic activities and sequences in the less developed world. Many years of work in this field have reinforced my confidence in the scope and effectiveness of economics in the most diverse institutional settings.

REFERENCES

Bauer, Peter. 1991. *The Development Frontier: Essays in Applied Economics.* Cambridge, Mass.: Harvard University Press.

Grassby, Richard. 1970. "English Merchant Capitalism in the Late Seventeenth Century." *Past & Present* 46: 87–107.

Hancock, William Keith. 1977. *Survey of British Commonwealth Affairs.* Westport, Conn.: Greenwood Press.

Mangat, J. S. 1969. *A History of the Asians in East Africa, 1886 to 1945.* Oxford: Clarendon Press.

McPhee, Allan. 1926. *The Economic Revolution in British West Africa.* London: G. Rutledge and Sons.

Meier, Gerald M. 1984. *Emerging from Poverty: The Economics That Really Matter.* New York: Oxford University Press.

Mui, Hoh-cheung, and Mui, Lorna H. 1989. *Shops and Shopkeeping in Eighteenth-Century England.* London: Routledge.

Price, Jacob M. 1989. "What Did Merchants Do? Reflections on British Overseas Trade, 1660–1790." *Journal of Economic History* 49: 267–84.

Rottenberg, Simon. 1953. "Note." *Review of Economics and Statistics* 35: 168–70.

Smith, Adam. 1776. *An Inquiry Into the Nature and Causes of the Wealth of Nations.* Dublin.

II

Disregard of Reality

ACCORDING to Hegel, the Owl of Minerva spreads its wings only at dusk. The later stages of one's career should be propitious for discerning tendencies and forces at work in society. Earlier preoccupations with specific studies can be helpful for subsequent reflection on wider issues but meanwhile absorb time and attention.

HIGH HOPES AND EMERGING DOUBTS

Like many of my contemporaries, fellow undergraduates and young academics alike, in my early days I expected much from economics, both in public policy and in intellectual interest. The great advances in the subject and the high intelligence of my academic colleagues seemed to confirm these hopes. Nevertheless, from about the early 1950s increasing claims for economics by its practitioners ran parallel with my own increasing doubts and reservations.

I came to realize for instance that economists systematically exaggerate the impact of their ideas. In an oft-quoted passage in *The General Theory*, Keynes insisted that in the long run the world is governed by little else than the ideas of economists and political philosophers. If this were true, the world would have enjoyed the benefits of free trade for at least one hundred years. Apart from being obviously unsustainable, Keynes's opinion is also naively parochial in attributing exclusive influence to the ideas of economists and political philosophers. He neglects the impact of the founders and leaders of religious movements, including the Buddha, Christ, Mohammed, and of military commanders such as Alexander the Great, Julius Caesar, and Napoleon.

The ideas of economists do affect the wider scene; like other ideas they have consequences. As Milton Friedman has reminded us, economists can suggest possible options to politicians. But we must not delude ourselves by overstating our influence, whether in the short period or over the longer run.

Well before my retirement I came to be increasingly perplexed by what was going on in economics. I observed, in particular, a widespread disregard of evident reality, in which I include neglect of basic propositions of the subject. Impressive advances coexisted with alarming retrogression.

This essay originally appeared in "Development Economics After 40 Years: Essays in Honor of Peter Bauer," *Cato Journal* [special issue] 7, no. 1 (spring/summer 1987).

UNEXPECTED TRANSGRESSIONS

It was in the 1950s that I first noticed the disregard of reality in economics. It was notable in two contexts: the dollar problem and the vicious circle of poverty.

For well over a decade in the 1940s and 1950s economists wrote about an indefinitely persistent and inescapable worldwide shortage of dollars. Some of these contributions and predictions were ostensibly sophisticated. In fact, they systematically ignored the rate of exchange, that is, the price of the dollar, as well as major determinants of this price such as interest rates and financial policy. This neglect of basics soon met the fate it deserved. In the later 1950s the shortage of dollars vanished and, indeed, was replaced by a glut. Many leading economists, and not just some amateurs and novices, had overlooked that supply of and demand for dollars depend on price.[1] This particular discussion subsided with the end of the dollar shortage. But its method of approach soon resurfaced in the idea, which is still with us, that poor countries face inescapable balance of payments difficulties.

The theory of the indefinite dollar shortage was not an example of tentative steps in the construction of exciting, and potentially fruitful, theorems or analytical instruments. Nor did the ostensibly elaborate analyses hinge on novel assumptions about expectations or dynamic processes. Rather, the episode was nothing but a serious transgression.

I now come to the vicious circle of poverty. According to this notion, stagnation and poverty are necessarily self-perpetuating: poor people generally and poor countries or societies in particular are trapped in their poverty and cannot generate sufficient savings to escape from the trap. This notion became a cornerstone of mainstream development economics. It was the signature tune of the advocates of foreign aid throughout the 1950s. Yet it is in obvious conflict with simple reality. Throughout history innumerable individuals, families, groups, societies, and countries—both in the West and the Third World—have moved from poverty to prosperity without external donations. All developed countries began as underdeveloped. If the notion of the vicious circle were valid, mankind would still be in the Stone Age at best.

These episodes also alerted me to the role of intellectual and political fashion in much of economics. Prominent, distinguished practitioners seem often to find it difficult to resist the vagaries and winds of fashion, even when these are ephemeral or blow them off course.

---

[1] Or more precisely, quantities supplied and demanded.

I have recently reread part of the literature of these two subjects with a mixture of incredulity, embarrassment, and amusement. It looked as if the queen of the social sciences was being dethroned by her entourage.

The two examples I have taken represent unequivocal examples of intellectual retrogression made possible by the disregard of reality. In the interwar years the role of the rate of exchange in the supply of and demand for currencies was routinely recognized. And before World War II, no one would have suggested that poor societies or countries were doomed to stagnation. Historians, anthropologists, administrators, and economists then discussed in detail the impact and implications of rapid changes in less developed countries (LDCs).

Alongside these instances of evident retrogression there took place major advances in economics, including advances in international trade theory and the theory of foreign exchanges, both closely related to the lapses.

There were dissenters from the most widely articulated opinion. This was particularly so in the case of the dollar problem, but applied also to the vicious circle. Some of the dissenters had high academic credentials, yet their views did not have much impact in academic circles and did not reach a wider public. This was because on the contemporary scene, also in academe, a voice is rarely effective without an echo. Dissenters find this difficult to secure unless their dissent is modish. The exponents of the dollar problem and the vicious circle of poverty, especially the latter, were supported and encouraged by articulate groups in the academies and the media. Dissent was crowded out.

These two episodes first prepared me to question received opinion, even when endorsed by the great and the good. Since the 1950s there has been an overdose of examples where reality is simply ignored or brushed aside.

Let me take a further example. Since World War II, many academics (as well as clerics, public figures, politicians, and spokesmen of the official international organizations) have argued that commercial contacts between the West and LDCs inflict economic damage on the peoples of the Third World. Sometimes it is said that Third World poverty is the result of Western neglect; but more often it is claimed that poverty results from Western oppression, exploitation, and manipulation of international trade. These widely canvassed opinions are not confined to Marxist-Leninists. (One should really say Leninists, since Marx was at times lyrical about the achievements of capitalism in transforming backward societies.) Yet as is abundantly evident throughout the Third World, the poorest and most backward societies and areas are those which have fewest commercial contacts with the West, and the most advanced are those with the most extensive and diversified contacts, including contacts with those bogeymen, the Western multinationals. Throughout the Third World the level of economic attainment declines as one moves away from regions with most Western contacts, to the aborigines and pygmies at the other end of the spectrum.

Those interested in the survival of ideas may like to know that the notions of the vicious circle of poverty and of the malign economic effects of commercial contacts with the West are alive and well.

ADVANCES IN ECONOMICS

Over the period in which I have been active in academic economics I have seen remarkable advances and also, as I have just noted, lapses which amount to blatant retrogression.

Advances in knowledge are what is expected from an academic discipline, especially when it has enjoyed a large expansion of resources and of opportunities. Even a necessarily incomplete list of significant advances must include various contributions to price theory, including the recognition of transaction costs; to the role and nature of the firm, including the economics of vertical integration; to the concept and implications of social cost; to the theory of international trade and the theory of the foreign exchanges; to the analysis of the diffusion and use of knowledge; to the economics of property rights; and to the economics of political and bureaucratic processes. Some of these advances have been helpful far outside economics and have been useful to historians, anthropologists, political scientists, and demographers.

Such advances go a long way to support the sanguine expectations of my early days. So do the intellectual capacity and technical competence of so many practitioners. My academic colleagues in recent years have been no less bright and competent than were most of my teachers a generation ago. If I am now perplexed, it is because I have encountered a plethora of instances of retrogression stemming from the disregard of reality.

The retrogressions are of a quite different order from what went on in economics in the past. The writings of nineteenth-century and early twentieth-century economists were often unsophisticated, even naive. But they were not in such evident conflict with reality as is so much of the more recent literature.

THE EMPEROR INVERTED

Mathematization of the subject has perhaps been the most conspicuous thread running through economics since I first entered it. In the 1930s one could read the journals without much knowledge of mathematics, with the exception only of *Econometrica* and the *Review of Economic Studies*. Today one is regarded as unqualified without some knowledge of mathematics, and especially of its language. As economics deals very largely with functional relationships and dynamic processes, some understanding of mathematics is undoubtedly valuable in many contexts ranging from the proper understanding of the concept of elasticity to the appreciation of feedback effects. And it is often convenient to express in mathematical form, inferences and conclusions derived from reasoning and empirical evidence. The appropriate procedure is, however, to reason to mathematics, rather than from mathematics. But as highly qualified practitioners have argued, mathematical methods and formulations have run riot in economics without proper appreciation of their limitations. The major limitations have been pointed out by outstanding scholars with technical mathematical credentials, including Marshall, Pigou, Keynes, Leontief, Stigler, and their observations have often been pointed, specific, and pertinent. Those of Norbert Wiener, one of the great figures of modern mathematics, were particularly vigorous. In one of my books I have referred at some length to his *God and Golem, Inc.*, published posthumously in 1964.[2] Yet these critical observations have made little impact. Reading the journals one gets the impression that economics has become little more than a branch of applied mathematics and one that can be successfully pursued with little reference to real-life phenomena.

Another conspicuous development in economics since I first studied the subject has been the use of econometric methods. Much useful work has been done with these methods. But far better qualified people than myself have demonstrated their frequent abuse and the misapplication or misinterpretation of their results.

Here I want to draw attention only to some of the ways in which mathematical economics and the use of econometrics have contributed to the disregard or neglect of evident reality. Their use has led to unwarranted concentration in economics on variables tractable to formal analysis. As a corollary, it has led to the neglect of influences which, even when highly pertinent, are not amenable to such treatment. Similarly, it has encouraged confusion between the significant, on the one hand, and the quantifiable (often only spuriously quantifiable), on the other. It has contributed to the neglect of background conditions and historical processes where they are indispensable for understanding. For instance, differences in income and wealth, both domestic and international, cannot be considered helpfully without attention to their antecedents and background.

Belief in the well-nigh universal applicability of testing by econometric methods has led to inappropriate claims for these methods. It has also

---

[2] See Bauer (1981, pp. 263–64), citing Wiener (1964).

smothered other forms of reasoning and inference. What has become of the traditional method of direct observation, reflection, tracing of connections, reaching tentative conclusions, and referring these back to observation and to established propositions of the discipline, or to findings of cognate disciplines? Such procedures are no less informative than quantitative analysis. For instance, with the traditional approaches the economist was much more likely to be aware of the gap between theoretical concepts and the available information.

The acceptance of quantitative methods as the most respectable procedure has permitted the burgeoning of incompetent or inappropriate econometric studies, including those based on seriously flawed data. Conversely, studies based on direct observation or detailed examination of slices of history are apt to be dismissed as anecdotal, unscholarly, or unscientific, even if they are informative. All too often their findings are dismissed as no more than casual empiricism or expressions of opinion. Moreover, in what passes for high-level discourse, insistence on the obvious can be made to sound trivial and therefore not worth saying. In short, preoccupation with mathematical and quantitative methods has brought with it a regrettable atrophy of close observation and simple reflection.

I have just asked the rhetorical question of what has happened in economics to the traditional sequence of observation, reflection, inference, tentative conclusion, and reference to established propositions, and to findings of other fields of study. Being rhetorical, the question can be answered readily. This type of reasoning and its vocabulary have contracted greatly throughout the subject and have virtually disappeared in large parts of it. And the traditional method has retreated not because it has been proved less informative than the methods that have replaced it. It has retreated because it has been castigated as being less rigorous than its more modish successors, largely because it less resembles the procedures of the natural sciences, especially those of physics.

I think that in the course of this shift of approach pertinent differences between the study of nature, especially physics, and economics have not been sufficiently recognized. Some differences may be only of degree, others are sufficiently pronounced to be more nearly differences in kind.

Natural scientists seek to establish uniformities about phenomena and relationships which are substantially invariant. Some of the phenomena and relationships studied by economists are also largely invariant. Others are not so constant, or at any rate their constant components are embedded in so many others that it is often difficult to discern the presence and extent of uniformities. Again, concepts and distinctions widely used by economists— or even regarded as basic—are imprecise, arbitrary, and shifting, and their real-life equivalents difficult to pin down: primary, secondary, and tertiary activity, or manufacturing and service activity; voluntary and involuntary unemployment; developed and underdeveloped countries; final and intermediate goods (a distinction that is critical for the definition of income); and many others. This extensive fuzziness of concepts and categories in economics limits informative use of mathematical methods: in mathematics the concepts and relationships, although completely abstract, are more precise and consistent.

For these various reasons, the methods for discerning uniformities, and their extent and limitations, differ considerably between the natural sciences, on the one hand—especially those like physics and chemistry that have been most successfully mathematicized—and social study, including economics on the other hand.[3] Some parts of economics, most obviously development economics, deal with events and sequences the informative study of which needs to incorporate practices from historical scholarship, such as reliance on primary sources, close observation, sustained reflection, the tracing of connections, and others.

These remarks on the differences between the study of nature and the study of society are not intended in the least to endorse the view that in economics, or social study generally, objective reasoning is impossible, which is another matter altogether. As I have written on this issue in a number of publications, I shall not develop it here and simply say that objective reasoning is quite as possible in economics as in the natural sciences.[4]

Mathematical methods often provide an effective facade or screen which covers or conceals empty formalism. They can camouflage disregard of basic propositions or simple evidence in models purporting to serve as basis for policy. Statistics, technical jargon, and sophisticated econometric techniques can also serve as a protective screen. But the use of mathematics is particularly effective because of the language barrier it provides. What we see is an inversion of the familiar Hans Andersen story of the Emperor's New Clothes. Here there *are* new clothes, and at times they are *haute couture*. But all too often there is no emperor within.

The achievements of mathematical economics and of econometric techniques have been secured at a great price. This price is not reflected adequately in the direct resource costs. In the book to which I have referred, Wiener insisted that the adoption of mathematical formulation and econometric methods involves misconceived imitation of the natural sciences; and also that it has enabled economists to remove both themselves and their public from the perception of reality.

---

[3] There is a large literature on this controversial subject. Apart from Wiener's short essay already mentioned, I have found particularly helpful the observations of Sir Peter Medawar (Nobel laureate biologist) in *The Art of the Soluble* (1967).

[4] See, for example, Bauer (1972, chap. 15; 1984, chap. 9).

THE WIDER SCENE

It is not surprising that indifference to reality is not confined to economics, but is extensive on the wider scene also. This divorce from reality is particularly baffling in view of well-nigh universal literacy in the West and the advances in the transmission of information. It is baffling also in view of the profound advances in science and technology. These latter subjects depend on reasoning which, although necessarily abstract, cannot fly in the face of reality.

Disregard of reality encompasses the refusal to accept the plain evidence of one's senses, neglect of simple connected reasoning, and the inability to recognize simple inconsistencies. What is behind all this?

Attempts to explain people's opinions always involve conjecture. Arguments can be assessed conclusively on the basis of logic or evidence. But why people accept or canvass them cannot be determined so confidently. In certain contexts some dominant influences are discernible. Many influences themselves represent a disregard of reality and also promote it; as in so many social situations, the process and the outcome are intertwined, even inseparable.

There are some who argue that there is nothing perplexing about conduct and opinions in evident conflict with reality, since they reflect no more than the promotion of self-interest. In this scheme of things apparently paradoxical and anomalous ideas and modes of conduct emerge from the operation of special interest groups or coalitions, including politicians, public servants, academics, and sections of the electorate. This factor can be significant.

Yet the operation of special interest groups cannot account for some conspicuous anomalies. Thus it can explain neither the hostility to the West in major international organizations nor the supine conduct of the West in them. Some of these organizations existed in embryonic form before World War II: the League of Nations in Geneva and the International Institute of Agriculture in Rome were precursors of today's UN and FAO. But their stances differed radically from what goes on there now. Moreover, the West supports lavishly and treats with deference African rulers who consistently vilify it. Such a stance by the West would have been unthinkable in the 1930s. These rulers have no votes in the West, nor do they advertise much in the media.

AMPUTATION OF THE TIME PERSPECTIVE

Confusion between advancement of knowledge and promotion of policy undoubtedly contributes to indifference to reality. This influence is certainly important in economics. That this is so is suggested by the profusion of transgressions against reality in those parts of the subject close to policy, such as development economics, the economics of Soviet-type planning, labor economics, the economics of poverty, and the economics of market failure. Some practitioners acknowledge the pursuit of political objectives; they also urge that in any event in social study objective reasoning is impossible. I may mention an experience of mine. On several occasions when my lectures criticized the notion of the vicious circle of poverty, members of the audience said that, whatever the validity of my criticisms, the notion was invaluable in the advocacy of foreign aid.

Much contemporary discourse is also afflicted by ignorance of the past and neglect of the time dimension in cultural and social phenomena. Sir Ernst Gombrich has termed this phenomenon the amputation of the time dimension from our culture. It has vitiated discourse in much of contemporary economics including, for example, mainstream development economics and the discussion of domestic and international income differences. In these and other parts of economics we cannot understand the situation we observe unless we know how it has arisen. For instance, the low income compared with the West in many LDCs with substantial exports of cash crops has often been adduced to support the contention that external contacts and the production of cash crops are not effective for economic progress, or indeed inhibit it. In fact, many cash-crop exporting countries have progressed very rapidly over the last century or less. But how can we expect societies, which in the late nineteenth century were still extremely backward, or even barbarous, to reach, within a few decades, the level of societies with many centuries, or even millennia, of economic development behind them? Another example is provided by changes in the distribution of income within a country. A higher degree of inequality may result, say, from a greater reduction in mortality among the poor (which would represent an improvement in their condition) or from the imposition of a regressive tax regime.

The factors behind the debilitating lack of the time perspective and neglect of evidently pertinent background include the speed of social and technical change and the multiplicity of messages reaching people, often about distant events. Very rapid and discontinuous social and technical change can unnerve and even unhinge people. There is only so much change that people can absorb as individuals, families, or societies. By disrupting sustained observation, these influences inhibit both connected thinking and the poise provided by background and time perspective.

Again, any inclination to equate the methods of natural science with those of the social sciences conduces to the downgrading or neglect of antecedents and processes. Whilst antecedents and processes are largely irrelevant in chemistry and physics, and wholly irrelevant in mathematics, they are critical for the understanding of social phenomena. The signal achievements of natural sciences and the pervasive results of their applications encourage habits of thought in social sciences based on misleading analogies between the two realms of study.

Whatever the factors behind them—and the list proposed here is both tentative and incomplete—lack of knowledge of the past and neglect of the time perspective are evident in much contemporary discourse. The resulting loss of collective memory has also opened the way for the manipulation and rewriting of history.

COLLECTIVE GUILT

The widespread or at any rate widely articulated feeling of guilt in the West is a significant influence behind some of the novel and baffling manifestations of the contemporary disregard of reality or even its denial. It helps to explain such matters as the acceptance of unfounded notions about Western responsibility for Third World backwardness and of the allegedly damaging effects of commercial contacts between the West and LDCs; the spineless conduct of the West toward African despots with negligible external power and resources, and the readiness of the West to support them in spite of their hostility to the West and in the face sometimes of inhuman domestic policies; and also the readiness of the West to finance international organizations that serve as forums for the embarrassment and undermining of the West. The guilt feeling in the West is reflected, for example, in the hostility toward South Africa. Whatever one may think of the conduct of the rulers there, they certainly treat their subjects no more harshly than various black rulers. As is well known, many people from black Africa are anxious to migrate to South Africa. The rulers of South Africa are singled out for special obloquy because they are white. Were they any color other than white, their conduct would arouse little or no comment in the West.

Again, the readiness to give aid to Asian and African rulers without questioning their policies reflects the same influence. Guilt-ridden people hope to assuage their feelings simply by giving away money (especially taxpayers' money) without questioning the results: what matters is to give away money, not what results from this process.

Although some elements of guilt feeling are part of the Judaeo-Christian tradition, guilt today is novel. Materially, the West has never had it so good, nor ever felt so bad about it. One reason for this is probably the failure of material prosperity to bring about the contentment and happiness so widely expected from it. Guilt has contributed to the confusion between the merits of charity in helping the less fortunate and the notion that income differences as such are reprehensible results of oppression and exploitation.

These differences are commonly referred to as inequalities or even as inequities. The confusion has been encouraged by an eagerness of churchmen to see themselves not as spiritual leaders but as social welfare workers or political activists.

Moreover, many influential opinion formers, including teachers, clerics, and people in the media, have come to dislike Western society, or even to hate it. They are apt both to harbor and to provoke feelings of guilt.

A major factor behind the emergence of contemporary collective guilt has been presumably the erosion of personal responsibility under the impact of social determinism. Participation in collective guilt has taken the place of individual responsibility. External forces are held responsible for personal misconduct and personal misfortune. And if we are all guilty, then no individual is.

Guilt feeling in Western societies has promoted indifference to reality, a loss of poise, and a loss of confidence. Loss of continuity and the amputation of the time perspective reinforce these effects of collective guilt. Kenneth Clark wrote that he was not sure what were all the necessary ingredients for civilization but he was sure that confidence and continuity were indispensable. Both have been seriously eroded in recent decades.

MISUSE OF LANGUAGE

In recent decades many thoughtful people have commented on the misuse of language, both in public discourse and in education. Disregard of reality promotes erosion of language, which promotes further disregard of reality. Language is to a culture or a society what money is to an economy; their erosion leads to a disintegration. Misuse of language covers the shifting interpretation of concepts such as socialism, equality, growth, monopoly, and many others. At times misuse of language is even acknowledged. If a country is officially designated as democratic or as a people's republic, we know that it is one in which people have no say in the government. Another category of examples is the treatment of countries and other collectivities as if they were single decision-making entities, or entities within which all the people have identical interests, experiences, and conditions. The aggregation of two-thirds of mankind as the Third World is a conspicuous example.

The growth of specialization, including long periods of specialized training, inhibits the exercise of critical faculty outside a narrow range and engenders disregard of reality in much academic and public discourse. This disregard is also facilitated by an understandable and rational reluctance of people to exercise their critical faculties in matters which affect them but about which they feel they can do little or nothing.

The vast expansion of information in recent decades may have been critical in the widespread atrophy of reflection. People, including academics, are expected to absorb so much information and technique that all too often they have little time, inclination, and capacity left for reflection and observation, even for simple assessment of the information reaching them.

The decline of traditional religious belief may also have conduced to a disregard of reality. This explanation could be appealing both to believers and to skeptics. Traditional religious belief provides a unified, coherent world view, the erosion of which enfeebles connected thinking. Conversely, it can be argued that the decline of religious belief diffuses the credulity of mankind over wide and more diverse areas. The speed of the decline reinforces such effects.

In this section and its three predecessors I have suggested some of the forces and influences behind the contemporary disregard of reality. I must remind the reader, however, that such suggestions are necessarily somewhat speculative. This is especially true of reflections on the varied and complex forces behind the Zeitgeist.

NEED TO RESTATE THE OBVIOUS

What has happened to us in the West for us to be so ready to fly in the face of reality and to reject the evidence of our senses? What makes us lose our poise and self-respect? It is as if amidst unprecedented prosperity and scientific achievement, inexplicable malevolent forces had undermined our mental and moral faculties.

The extensive and baffling indifference to reality matters greatly. Among other results, it has undermined standards in parts of economics, in other social studies, and in wider areas of ostensibly serious discourse. It is reversion to barbarism. Ortega y Gasset wrote that the absence of standards is the essence of barbarism. It is because this condition prevails in parts of economics alongside its great achievements of recent decades that I am now so baffled by the present state of the subject.

The tendency to disregard simple realities has undermined the poise, self-assurance, and stance of the West in the international arena. It has also underpinned the uncritical acceptance of ideas and policies damaging to the West, and much more so to the peoples of the Third World. This is not surprising. Polities and societies bent on disregarding reality must be vulnerable to adversity and also to threats from within and without.

Such concerns highlight the perceptiveness of two observations by authors widely separated in time and very different in general outlook. Their observations make a fitting conclusion to this essay. Pascal wrote in the seventeenth century: "Let us labour at trying to think clearly: herein lies the source of moral conduct" [Travaillons donc à penser bien: voilà le principe de la morale]. And in our own time George Orwell wrote: "We have sunk to such a depth that the restatement of the obvious has become the first duty of intelligent men."

REFERENCES

Bauer, Peter T. 1972. *Dissent on Development*. Cambridge: Harvard University Press.

————. 1981. *Equality, the Third World, and Economic Delusion*. Cambridge: Harvard University Press.

————. 1984. *Reality and Rhetoric*. Cambridge: Harvard University Press.

Medawar, Peter. 1967. *The Art of the Soluble*. London: Methuen.

Wiener, Norbert. 1964. *God and Golem, Inc.* Cambridge: MIT Press.

III

The Land and the People

IT IS widely held that the most important cause of poverty lies in the relationship between land and people, that is, in scarcity of land or exploitation of cultivators. This is not so. For instance, amidst abundant land and vast natural resources, the American Indians before Columbus remained wretchedly poor, without domestic animals and without even the wheel when much of Europe with far less land was already rich and had developed a very high culture. Incidentally, before Cortez the Aztecs commended in the show were very poor and practiced large-scale human sacrifice, which was not good for living standards, especially those of the victims.

Nor is the present Third World short of natural resources. Most of Africa and Latin America and much of Asia is sparsely populated. Many millions of extremely poor people have abundant cultivable land. Neither shortage of land nor exploitation accounts for the famines in thinly populated African countries such as Ethiopia and Tanzania. Even in India much land is officially classified as uncultivated but usable. The small size and low productivity of farms in much of the Third World reflect the want not of land but of ambition, energy, and skill, which also explains the low level of productive capital.

Before the mid–nineteenth century, when many of them had already become rich, Jews and nonconformists in Europe had neither land nor political rights. Again, the poor, illiterate Chinese immigrants in prewar Malaya were largely barred from owning land, but they nevertheless greatly outdistanced not only the privileged Malays but also the immigrant Indians— one of many examples of group differences in economic performance.

Sustained prosperity owes little or nothing to natural resources—witness, in the past, Holland, much of it drained from the sea by the seventeenth century; Venice, a wealthy world power built on a few mud flats; and now West Germany, Switzerland, Japan, Singapore, Hong Kong, and Taiwan, to cite only the most obvious instances of prosperous countries very short of land and natural resources, but evidently not short of human resources.

If poverty were inherently self-perpetuating, as is often argued and also suggested in the show, countless people would not have risen from poverty to riches all over the world, conspicuously so in the United States and the Far East.

Critical commentary on Galbraith's public television series, *The Age of Uncertainty*.

Nor do income differences normally reflect exploitation, but differences in performance. Income and wealth are usually earned or produced, not extracted from other people by depriving them of what they had, or could have had. The way to look at income differences is this: some people and societies have emerged from the surrounding sea of poverty sooner or to a greater extent than have others, but the earlier emergence of the former helps rather than obstructs the performance and prospects of the latter.

Economic performance depends on personal, cultural, and political factors, on people's aptitudes, attitudes, motivations, and social and political institutions. Where these are favorable, capital will be generated locally or attracted from abroad, and if land is scarce, food will be obtained by intensive farming or by exporting other goods.

Poverty and prosperity are not usually matters of land. Poverty or riches and personal and social satisfaction depend on man, on his culture, and on his political arrangements. Understand *that*, and you understand the most important cause of wealth or deprivation.

IV

Population Explosion: Disaster or Blessing

THE twenty-third General Population Conference of The International
Union for the scientific study of population which met in Beijing in October 1997 focused on overpopulation as a serious threat to human survival
and a major cause of poverty. Warren Buffet, Bill Gates, corporations, governments, and international organizations are dedicating and promising to
dedicate enormous resources to reverse the threat of overpopulation. But
is there any correlation between population density and poverty?

Poverty in the Third World is not caused by population growth or pressure. Economic achievement and progress depend on people's conduct,
not on their numbers. Population growth in the Third World is not a major threat to prosperity. The crisis is invented. The central issue of policy is
whether the number of children should be determined by the parents or
by agents of the state.

Since World War II it has been widely argued that population growth is
a major, perhaps decisive, obstacle to the economic progress and social
betterment of the underdeveloped world, the majority of mankind. Thus
Robert S. McNamara, former president of the World Bank, wrote:

> To put it simply: the greatest single obstacle to the economic and social ad-
> vancement of the majority of peoples in the underdeveloped world is rampant
> population growth. . . .
>
> The threat of unmanageable population pressures is very much like the
> threat of nuclear war. . . .

I could easily multiply such examples.

These apprehensions rest primarily on three assumptions. The first is that
national income per head measures economic well-being. The second is
that economic performance and progress depend critically on land and
capital per head. The third is that people in the Third World are ignorant
of birth control or careless about family size: they procreate regardless of
consequences. A subsidiary or supporting assumption is that population
trends in the Third World can be forecast with accuracy for decades ahead.

Conflicting views on mankind are discernible behind these assumptions
and, indeed, behind debates on population. One view envisages people as

This lecture was originally given at Princeton University, December 1997. A revised version of the lecture was delivered at the Cato Institute, Washington, D.C., 19 October 1994.

deliberate decision-making persons in matters of family size. The other view treats people as being under the sway of uncontrollable sexual urges, their numbers limited only by forces outside themselves, either Malthusian checks of nature or the power of superior authority. However, proponents of both views agree that LDC governments, urged by the West, should encourage or, if necessary, force people to have smaller families.

Suppose for the moment that an increase in population reduced income per head, a matter to which I shall return later. Such a reduction need not mean that the well-being of either families or the wider community had been reduced.

National income per head is usually regarded as an index of economic welfare, even of welfare as such. The use of this index raises major problems, such as demarcation between inputs and outputs in both production and consumption (e.g., the cost of travel to work or to shops).

In the economics of population, national income per head founders completely as a measure of welfare. It ignores satisfaction people derive from having children or from living longer. The birth of a child immediately reduces income per head for the family and also for the country as a whole. The death of the same child has the opposite effect. Yet for most people, the first event is a blessing, the second a tragedy. Ironically, the birth of a child is registered as a reduction in national income per head, while the birth of a calf shows up as an improvement.

The wish of the great majority of mankind to have children has extended across centuries, cultures, and classes. This is evident from the survival of the human race: most people have been ready to bear the cost of raising two or more children to the age of puberty. Widely held ideas and common attitudes reflect and recognise the benefits parents expect from having children. The biblical injunction is to "be fruitful and multiply." Less well known in the West is the traditional greeting addressed to brides in India, "May you be the mother of eight sons."

The uniformly unfavourable connotation of the term *barren* reflects the same sentiment. The practice of adoption in some countries also indicates the desire for children. All this refutes the notion that children are simply a cost or burden.

Some have argued that high birthrates in LDCs, especially among the poorest, result in lives so wretched as to be not worth living: that over a person's life, suffering or disutility may exceed utility. If this were so, fewer such lives would increase the sum total of happiness. This view implies that external observers are qualified to assess the joys and sorrows of others. It implies that life and survival are of no value to the people involved. This outlook, which raises far-reaching ethical issues, is unlikely to be morally acceptable to most people, least of all as basis for forcible action to restrict people's reproductive behaviour, especially when it is remembered how widely it was espoused about the poor in the West only about two generations ago. Nor is this opinion consistent with simple observation, which suggests that even very poor people prefer to live rather than not to live, as is shown by their striving to remain among the living by, for instance, seeking medical help to prolong their lives.

Thus these considerations make clear that the much-deplored population explosion of recent decades is seen more appropriately as a blessing rather than as a disaster because it reflects a fall in mortality, which is an improvement in people's welfare not a deterioration.

Much of the advocacy of state-sponsored birth control is predicated on the implicit assumptions that people in high-fertility Third World countries do not know about contraceptives and that they do not take into account the long-term consequences of their actions. Most people in the Third World do know about birth control and practice it. In the Third World, fertility is well below fecundity; that is, the number of actual births is well below the biologically possible number. Traditional methods of birth control were widely practiced in societies much more backward than contemporary Third World countries.

Over most of the Third World cheap Western-style consumer goods have been conspicuous for decades while condoms, intrauterine devices, and the Pill have so far spread only very slowly. All this suggests that the demand for modern contraceptives has been small because people either do not want to restrict their families or prefer other ways of doing so.

It follows that the children are generally wanted by their parents. It is of course true, especially in Catholic or Muslim societies, that a woman may not want many children but has to bow to the wishes of her husband. Any attempt to enforce changes in mores in such societies raises issues that I cannot pursue here. In any case, my argument in this essay is not affected by this issue.

Children are certainly avoidable. And people in LDCs generally are not ignorant of the long-term consequences of their actions. Indeed, young women often say that they want more children and grandchildren to provide for them in their old age. The readiness to take the long view is also evident in other decisions such as the planting of slow-maturing trees or embarking on long-distance migration.

I now have to consider a range of questions known in economics as externalities. The first question here is whether parents bear the full cost of having and raising their children. If they did not bear these costs fully, then they would have more children than they would otherwise. According to the usual assumption of welfare economics, the satisfaction of the parents from the additional children would be less than the weight of the burden falling on others. It is often assumed that parents in the Third World do not bear the full costs of having children, in particular the costs of health care and education, and that a substantial part of those costs is in fact borne by taxpayers. The particular costs are unlikely to be heavy in LDCs. They are likely to be lower relative to the national income than in the West. For instance, schools are often simple, inexpensive structures. For social and institutional reasons, basic health services are extensively performed by medical auxiliaries and nurses rather than by fully qualified doctors. If the adverse externalities were such as to call for remedial action, this should take the form of changes in the volume, direction, and financing of the relevant public expenditures, and not for imposed reductions in family size.

The extended family provides a further example of the same negative externality. Parents may have more children if they know that part of the cost is borne by other members of their extended family. However, as just noted, the burden falling on others is likely to be small. Moreover, the extended family is embodied in the mores of much of the less developed world. And any effect of the operation in this context of the extended family will diminish or disappear if the extended family system gives way with modernization, a matter examined in the concluding section of this essay.

Congestion in cities is at times instanced as an adverse externality resulting from population growth. But the rapid growth of these cities derives from the pull of these cities especially the capitals. This in turn reflects the limitations to many people of rural life and from the higher incomes and other benefits available or expected in the cities. The income differences are increased when rural earnings are depressed as a result of policies benefiting the urban population. That the growth of large cities is the result of these influences is evidenced by large conurbations in sparsely populated LDCs, such as Brazil and Zaire, and generally by the more rapid increase in the urban populations of LDCs than in the country as a whole. In any case, undesirable crowding in large cities is not a function of their size or growth, much less of the growth of the national population: it is the inevitable consequence of the pricing of housing and transport, unrelated to the scarcity of these resources.

Similar considerations apply to other supposed adverse external effects of population growth on the environment, including deforestation, soil erosion, and depletion of fish stocks. The rate of use of such assets can be adjusted by pricing and the assignment of property rights.

Altogether, it is highly unlikely that population growth would set up major adverse externalities, let alone externalities that would warrant the exercise of pressure on people to have fewer children.

The practically exclusive preoccupation with possible adverse externalities of population growth is unwarranted. Population growth often has favourable external effects. It can facilitate the more effective division of labour and thereby increase real incomes. In fact, in much of Southeast Asia, Africa, and Latin America, sparseness of population inhibits economic advance. It retards the development of transport facilities and communications and thus inhibits the movement of people and goods and the spread of new ideas and methods. These obstacles to enterprise and economic advance are particularly difficult to overcome.

At the later stage of development, there are also significant positive externalities arising from greater scope for the division of labour in economic activity in science, technology, and research generally.

As I shall argue later, even if it could be shown that adverse externalities are significant and outweigh the positive externalities, this would call for policies quite different from pressure on parents to have fewer children.

Thus, population growth is unlikely to reduce welfare; we can now consider whether it is likely to reduce conventionally measured income per head. It seems prima facie commonsensical that prosperity depends on natural resources—namely land and mineral resources—and also capital and that population growth reduces the per capita supply of these determinants of income. Indeed, if nothing else changed, an increase in population must reduce income per head: and this must be true in the very short run. However, this simple analysis reveals nothing about developments over a longer period. Then, other influences affecting productivity become significant, other influences that can be elicited or reinforced by an increase in population. These influences include the spread of knowledge, division of labour, changes in attitudes and habits, redeployment of resources, and technical change. Economic analysis, in short, cannot demonstrate that an increase in population must entail reduction in income per head over a longer period.

There is ample evidence that rapid population growth has certainly not inhibited economic progress in either the West or the contemporary Third World. The population of the Western world has more than quadrupled since the middle of the eighteenth century. Real income per head is estimated to have increased fivefold at least. Much of the increase in incomes took place when population increased as fast as in most of the contemporary less developed world, or even faster.

Similarly, population growth in the Third World has often gone hand in hand with rapid material advance. In the 1890s, Malaya was a sparsely populated area of hamlets and fishing villages. By the 1930s, it had become a country with large cities, extensive commerce, and extensive plantation and mining operations. The total population rose through natural increase and immigration from about one and a half million to about six million, and the number of Malays increased from about one million to about two and half million. The much larger population had much higher material standards and lived longer than the small numbers of the 1890s. Since World War II a number of LDCs have combined rapid population increase with rapid, even spectacular economic growth for decades on end, for example, Taiwan, Hong Kong, Malaysia, Kenya, the Ivory Coast, Mexico, Colombia, and Brazil.

Conventional views on population growth assume that endowments of land and other natural resources are critical for economic performance. This assumption is refuted by experience in both the distant and more recent past. And there is much additional evidence that works in the same direction. Amid abundant land, the American Indians before Columbus were extremely backward at a time when most of Europe, with far less land, was already advanced. Europe in the sixteenth and seventeenth centuries included prosperous Holland, much of it reclaimed from the sea, and Venice, a wealthy world power built on a few mud flats. At present, many millions of poor people in the Third World live amid ample cultivable land. Indeed, in much of Southeast Asia, Central Africa, and interior of Latin America, land is a free good. Conversely, land is now very expensive in both Hong Kong and Singapore, probably the most densely populated countries in the world with originally very poor land. For example, Hong Kong in the 1840s consisted largely of eroded hillsides, and much of Singapore in the nineteenth century was empty marsh land. Both these countries are now highly industrialized and prosperous communities. The experience of other countries in both the East and the West points in the same direction. Poor countries differ in density. For example, India's population density is some 750 people per square mile, while Zaire's density is approximately 40 people per square mile. And prosperous countries differ in density. Japan's density is some 850 people per square mile, while U.S. density is approximately 70 people per square mile. All these instances underline the obvious: the importance of people's economic qualities and of the policies of governments.

It is pertinent also that productivity of the soil in both prosperous and poor countries owes very little to the "original and indestructible powers of the soil," that is, to land as a factor in totally inelastic supply. The productivity of land is the result largely of human activity: labour, investment, science, and technology.

The wide differences in economic performance and prosperity between individuals and groups in the same country with access to the same natural resources also make clear that the availability of natural resources cannot be critical to economic achievement. Such differences have been, and still are, conspicuous the world over. Salient examples of group differences in the same country are those among Chinese, Indians, and Malays in Malaysia; Chinese and others elsewhere in Southeast Asia; Parsees, Jains, Marwaris, and others in India; Greeks and Turks in Cyprus; Asians and Africans in East and Central Africa; Ibo and others in Nigeria; and Chinese, Lebanese, and West Indians in the Caribbean. The experience of Huguenots, Jews, and nonconformists in the West also makes clear that natural resources are not critical for economic achievement. For long periods, these prosperous groups were either not allowed to own land or had their access to it severely restricted.

Mineral resources have often yielded substantial windfalls to those who discovered or developed them or expropriated their owners. Latin American gold and silver in the sixteenth century and the riches of contemporary oil-producing states are often cited as examples of prosperity conferred by natural resources. But the precious metals of the Americas did not promote economic progress in pre-Columbian America, nor did their capture ensure substantial development in Spain. The oil reserves of the Middle East and elsewhere were worthless until discovered and developed by the West, and it must be conjectural whether they will lead to sustained economic advance.

Population growth as such can induce changes in economic behaviour favourable to capital formation. The parents of enlarged families may well work harder and save more in order to provide for the future of their families. Poor people in LDCs, as in the West, save and invest. For instance, they can sacrifice leisure for work or transfer their labour and land to more productive use, perhaps by replacing subsistence production by cash crops. Poor and illiterate traders have often accumulated capital by working harder and opening up local markets.

It is often thought that population growth brings about certain special problems such as famine, exhaustion of mineral resources, and large-scale unemployment.

There is no danger that malnutrition or starvation through shortage of land will arise from population growth. Contemporary famines and food shortages occur mostly in sparsely populated subsistence economies such as Ethiopia, the Sahel, Tanzania, Uganda, and Zaire. In these countries land is abundant and, in some places, even a free good. Recurrent food shortages or famines in these and other LDCs reflect features of subsistence and near-subsistence economies such as nomadic style of life, shifting cultivation, and inadequate communications and storage facilities. These conditions are exacerbated by lack of public security, official restrictions on the activities of traders, restrictions on the movement of food, and restrictions on imports of both consumer goods and farm supplies. Unproductive forms of land tenure such as tribal systems of land rights can also bring about shortages. No famines are reported in such densely populated regions of the less developed world as Taiwan, Hong Kong, Singapore, western Malaysia, and the cash-crop–producing areas of West Africa. Indeed, where a greater density of population in sparsely populated countries brings about improved transport facilities and greater public security, it promotes emergence from subsistence production.

There is no reason why population growth should lead to unemployment. A large population means more consumers as well as more producers. The large increase in population in the West over the last two centuries has not brought about persistent mass unemployment. Substantial unemployment emerged when population growth was already much slower in the twentieth century than it had been in the nineteenth. And when in the 1930s and 1940s an early decline in population was widely envisaged, this was generally thought to portend more unemployment because a decline in population would reduce the mobility and adaptability of the labour force and would also diminish the incentive to invest.

Contemporary experience in the less developed world confirms that rapid increase in population does not result in unemployment and also that the issue cannot be discussed simply on the basis of numbers and physical resources. Until recently, population grew very rapidly in densely populated Hong Kong and Singapore without resulting in unemployment. There is far less land per head in Singapore than in neighbouring Malaysia; yet many people move from Malaysia to Singapore in search of employment and higher wages, both as short-term and long-term migrants and as permanent settlers.

The idea that population growth results in unemployment implies that labour cannot be substituted for land or capital in particular activities and also that resources cannot be moved from less labour-intensive to more labour-intensive activities. The idea implies that the elasticity of substitution between labour and other resources is zero in both production and consumption. That this is not so is shown by the development of more intensive forms of agriculture in many LDCs, including the development of double and treble cropping. Substitution in consumption is evidenced by the frequent changes in patterns of consumption.

Dramatic long-term population forecasts are often put forward with much confidence. Such confidence is unwarranted. It is useful to recall the population forecasts of the 1930s and 1940s when a substantial decline of population, primarily in the West but to some extent worldwide, was widely predicted. Articles by prominent academics appeared under such headings as "The End of the Human Experiment" and "The Suicide of the Human Race."

Within less than one human generation, the population problem has come to mean the exact opposite of what it was formerly held to be. The earlier scare of a decline has come to be replaced by the scare of an increase, primarily in LDCs. The scare has remained, but the sign has been reversed from minus to plus. There are even now, along with predictions of over-population, predictions of depopulation since the fertility rate of many parts of the world is below replacement level and this trend might be spreading as countries are Westernised.

As in the 1930s and 1940s, the predictions put forward so confidently are accompanied by far-reaching proposals for dealing with the supposed problem. In reality only the roughest forecasts of population trends in the

Third World are warranted. The basis for confident predictions for the Third World, or even for individual LDCs, is far more tenuous than it was for the forecasts of long-term population trends in the West in the 1930s and 1940s that proved so unsuccessful.

In much of the Third World there is no registration of births and deaths, and, even where there is, it is often incomplete. Estimates of the population of African countries differ as much as one-third or more, and for large countries, such as Nigeria, this means tens of millions of people. Estimates of the population of the People's Republic of China, the most populous country in the world, also differ substantially.

In the coming decades, major political, cultural, and economic changes will occur in much of the Third World. These changes are unpredictable, and so are people's responses. For instance, contrary to expectations, the economic improvement in recent decades in some Third World countries has resulted in higher not lower fertility. Similarly, decline in mortality in many LDCs has not been accompanied by a decline in fertility that had been widely expected in the belief that people had many children to replace those who died young. Moreover, in some of these countries urban and rural fertility rates are about the same while in others there are wide differences. The relationship of fertility to social class and occupation is also much more varied in the Third World than in the West.

These considerations should put into perspective such widely canvassed and officially endorsed practices as forecasting to the nearest million the population of the world for the year 2000 or beyond.

There is one demographic relationship of considerable generality that bears upon population trends in LDCs. Professor Caldwell, a leading Australian demographer, has found that systematic restriction of family size in the Third World is practiced primarily by women who have adopted Western attitudes toward childbearing and childrearing, as a result of exposure to Western education, media, and contacts. Their attitude to fertility control does not depend on income, status, or urbanisation, but on Westernisation. In this context, Westernisation means the readiness of parents to forgo additions to family income from the work of young children and also to incur increased expenditure on education, which reflects greater concern with the material welfare of their children.

Caldwell's conclusion is more plausible and more solidly based than the widely held view that higher incomes lead to reduced fertility. It is true that in the West and in the Westernised parts of the Third World higher incomes and lower fertility are often, though by no means always, associated. But it is not the case that higher incomes and smaller families reflect greater ambition for material welfare for oneself and one's family. Both, in other words, reflect a change in motivation. By contrast, when parental incomes are increased as a result of subsidies or windfalls, without a change in attitudes, the parents are likely to have more children, not fewer. This last point is pertinent to the proposals of many Western observers who, without recognising the contradiction, urge both population control and also more aid to poor people with large families.

Some broad, unambitious predictions of Third World population prospects may be in order. Although the speed and extent of Westernisation are uncertain, the process is likely to make some headway. The result would be some decline in fertility. But the large proportion of young people and the prevailing reproductive rates will ensure significant increases in population in the principal regions of the Third World over the next few decades. Population growth in the Third World as a whole is unlikely to fall much below 2 percent and may for some years continue around 2.5 percent, the rough estimate of growth rates in the 1980s. It is therefore likely to remain considerably higher than in the West, Japan, and Australasia.

If this difference in population growth continues, then the population of the West, Japan, and Australasia will, over the years, shrink considerably relative to that of Asia, Africa, and Latin America. This will have wide political and cultural consequences. But I cannot explore these consequences in an essay on the relation between population growth and economic attainment and well-being—not on the ethnic, racial, or national composition of mankind.

We have seen that it is most unlikely that Third World population growth could be such as to jeopardize the well-being of families and societies. But if this well-being were for any reason to be seriously impaired by population growth, reproductive behaviour would change without official pressure. There is, therefore, no cause for trying to force people to have fewer children than they would like. And when such pressure emanates from outside the local culture it is especially objectionable. It is also likely to provoke resistance to modernisation generally.

The central issue in population policy, then, is whether the number of children people may have should be decided by individuals and families or by politicians and national and international civil servants.

Advocates of officially sponsored population policies often argue that they do not propose compulsion but intend only to extend the options of people by assisting the spread of knowledge about contraceptive methods. As I have argued, people in LDCs usually know about both traditional and more modern methods of birth control. Moreover, in many Third World countries, especially in Asia and Africa, official information, advice, and persuasion in practice often shade into coercion. In most of these societies people are more subject to authority than in the West. And especially in recent years, the incomes and prospects of many people have come to depend heavily on official favours. In India, for example, promotion in the civil service, allocation of driving and vehicle licences, and access to subsidised credit, official housing, and other facilities have all been linked at times to restriction of family size. Forcible mass sterilisation, which took place in India in the 1970s, and the extensive coercion in the People's Republic of China are only extreme cases in a spectrum of measures extending from publicity to compulsion.

Policies and measures pressing people to have fewer children can provoke acute anxiety and conflict, and they raise serious moral and political problems. Implementation of such policies may leave people dejected and inert, uninterested in social and economic advance or incapable of achieving it. Such outcomes have often been observed when people have been forced to change their mores and conduct.

There is one type of official policy that would tend to reduce population growth, extend the range of personal choice, and simultaneously promote attitudes and mores helpful to an improvement of the well-being of the population and also to economic advance. This policy is the promotion of external commercial contacts of people of LDCs, especially their contacts with the West. Such contacts have been powerful agents of voluntary change in attitudes and habits, particularly in the erosion of those harmful to economic improvement. Throughout the less developed world, the most prosperous groups and areas are those with most external commercial contacts. And such contacts also encourage voluntary reduction of family size. Thus, extension of such contacts and the widening of people's range of choice promote both economic advance and reduction in fertility. In these circumstances, the reduction in family size is achieved without the damaging effects of official pressure on people in their most private and vital concerns. Yet this type of policy is not on the agenda of advocates of the need for fewer children in LDCs.

It is widely agreed that the West should not impose its standards, mores, and attitudes on Third World governments and peoples. Yet, ironically, the most influential voices call for the exact opposite when it comes to population control.

V

Foreign Aid: Abiding Issues

FOREIGN AID is demonstrably neither necessary nor sufficient to promote economic progress in the so-called Third World and is indeed much more likely to inhibit economic advance than it is to promote it. This is so because the inflow of foreign aid sets up major adverse effects on the factors behind economic progress. This has been so since the beginning of foreign aid. In recent years the adverse effects have been compounded by the practice of linking foreign aid to government policies to promote birth control in the mistaken belief that population growth is a major cause of Third World poverty.

THE AXIOMATIC APPROACH TO AID

Since the early years after World War II, subsidies in the form of grants or soft loans from governments of relatively rich to those of relatively poor countries have been accepted elements in international relations. This policy is known as foreign aid in the United States and as development aid elsewhere.

Foreign aid emerged in the late 1940s. Since then it has expanded from a few hundred million U.S. dollars a year to well over $50 billion a year by the 1990s. In the early days leading advocates of this policy argued that expenditure of a few hundred million dollars a year over a relatively short period would be sufficient to ensure what was then called self-sustaining growth in the recipient countries so that aid would then be discontinued. Some forty years and hundreds of billions of dollars later the indefinite continuation of this policy is taken for granted. Foreign aid has become a regularly accepted component of Western government budgets.

Some of the resolutions at the 1992 United Nations conference on the environment (the Rio Conference) envisage many additional official transfers from the West to the Third World for a variety of purposes, especially environmental protection and more effective population control. The 1995 UN Summit at Copenhagen, known as the UN Poverty Summit or Social Summit, again envisaged further large-scale transfers from the West to the Third World.

Wide extension of the scope of this policy of intergovernmental subsidies is already in process. Large official subsidies to the postcommunist govern-

This lecture was given at New York University, December 1996.

ments of Russia and Eastern Europe have already been granted and further amounts are under discussion. Arrangements for administering and distributing these subsidies are already in place.

To call official wealth transfers "aid" promotes an unquestioning attitude. It disarms criticism, obscures realities, and prejudges results. Who can be against aid to the less fortunate? The term has enabled aid supporters to claim a monopoly of compassion and to dismiss critics as lacking in understanding and compassion.

However, the term foreign aid is now so widely used that it is not possible to avoid it. I shall use interchangeably the terms transfers, subsidies, and aid, and occasionally refer to aid-recipient countries. But it should always be remembered that most of official aid goes to governments not to the destitute people shown in aid propaganda.

In this essay I shall be concerned with the operation of aid from the West to Third World countries. Most of the argument applies also to Western subsidies to Russia and Eastern Europe and also to the transfers from higher income to lower income states of the European Union.

The effects of foreign aid cannot be inferred simply from the budgetary spending by the donors. It is foreign aid which has brought into existence the Third World (also called the South) and which thus underlies the so-called North-South dialogue or confrontation. Foreign aid is a source of the North-South conflict, not its solution. Take away foreign aid, and there is no Third World or South as aggregate. A further pervasive consequence of aid has been to promote or exacerbate the politicisation of life in aid-receiving countries. These major results have been damaging to both the West and the peoples of the less developed world.

An unquestioning attitude prevails widely in public discussion of this policy. Discussions on this subject in legislatures, especially in Europe, are not debates but are akin to seminars of like-minded aid supporters or enthusiasts.

SOME CONSPICUOUS ANOMALIES

The uncritical attitude towards foreign aid can be illustrated by some episodes both tragic and bizarre. In June 1982 at the height of the Falklands War the British government openly supplied aid to the Argentine government under a United Nations programme, even though Argentina was using expensive and sophisticated weaponry, against British forces, without this aid evoking any protest.

The government of Iraq, which enjoyed huge oil revenues in the 1980s, also received many millions of dollars of Western aid annually throughout this period, which facilitated the build-up of its vast military arsenal.

Western aid has routinely gone to governments hostile to the donors, whom they embarrass and thwart whenever they can. Examples range from Nkrumah's Ghana in the 1950s to Nyerere's Tanzania and Mengistu's Ethiopia in the 1980s.

AID WITHOUT STRINGS?

One persistent anomaly of these subsidies has been especially harmful to the peoples in the recipient countries. This has been the maintenance or expansion of subsidies in the face of destructive official policies.

The Western subsidies have been continued or increased when the recipients pursued policies extremely damaging to their own subjects, including the poorest. The long list of such policies includes persecution of the most productive groups, especially ethnic minorities, and sometimes their expulsion; suppression of trade, and at times destruction of the trading system; restriction on the inflow of foreign capital and enterprises; extensive confiscation of property including forced collectivisation; voluntary or enforced purchase of foreign enterprises which absorbs scarce capital and deprives the country of valuable skills; price policies that discourage agricultural production; expensive forms of support of unviable activities and projects, including subsidised import substitution; and the imposition of specific economic controls which, among other adverse effects, restrict external contacts and domestic mobility and so retard the spread of new ideas and methods.

From their inception, the subsidies have been geared largely to the per capita incomes in the recipient countries and occasionally also to their balance-of-payments difficulties. Major components of Western aid, such as British aid and aid distributed by IDA (the International Development Association, a World Bank affiliate) are targeted primarily towards governments of countries with very low per capita incomes. To support rulers on the criterion of the poverty of their subjects does nothing to discourage policies of impoverishment or even immiseration and may even encourage them.

Many aid-recipient governments have persecuted and even expelled some of the most productive groups, including Chinese in Southeast Asia or Asians and Europeans in Africa. On the criterion of poverty, such governments qualify for larger subsidies because incomes in their countries are now lower. A similar situation exists when a government restricts the employment opportunities of women in the name of Islamic fundamentalism.

Large-scale spending by aid recipients on armaments is familiar, though its extent less so. In 1981 (at the height of the so-called Cold War between the superpowers) the German Aid Ministry estimated that Third World governments then accounted for about one-fifth of total world spending on armaments. This spending was largely on arms intended for use either against their own subjects or against other aid recipients.

Import restrictions by donor countries against exports from the recipients of their largesse is a familiar paradox. It is explained by the operations of influential lobbies for these subsidies in both donor and recipient countries and similar lobbies behind the import restrictions in the donor countries. There is no effective lobby for freer trade.

ARGUMENTS AND JUSTIFICATIONS

The process by which the case for official aid has come to be regarded as self-evident has been gradual. From about the 1950s to about the 1970s advocates of this policy often still found it necessary to put forward arguments or justifications, some of which still frequently surface in discussions on this subject.

Much the most persistent argument for these subsidies has always been that without external donations poor countries cannot emerge from poverty. Since about the late 1970s another argument has become prominent, namely that the subsidies are required to improve the condition of the poorest peoples in the Third World.

External subsidies were deemed indispensable for the progress of poor countries because they could not themselves generate the capital required for their advance. This argument, popularised as the vicious circle of poverty and stagnation, was the central theme of development economics from the 1940s to the 1970s. It is still often heard, notably in the context of official assistance to postcommunist governments. This argument was endorsed by for instance Nobel Laureates Gunnar Myrdal and Paul Samuelson. The latter formulated it concisely: "They (the backward nations) cannot get their heads above water because their production is so low that they can spare nothing for capital formation by which the standard of living could be raised."

In reality, throughout the world and throughout history, countless individuals, families, groups, communities, and countries have emerged from poverty to prosperity without donations and often did so within a few years or decades. Immigrant communities such as those of Southeast Asia and North America are familiar examples. The hypothesis is also disproved by the existence of developed countries, all of which started poor and developed without subsidies. If external subsidies were indispensable for economic advance, mankind would still be living in the Old Stone Age. The world is a closed system that has never received subsidies from outside itself.

Recent examples of emergence from backwardness and poverty in a few decades without subsidies are readily observable in what is nowadays called the Third World. Since about the 1860s large parts of the underdeveloped world, such as Southeast Asia, West Africa, and Latin America, were transformed in a few decades without subsidies.

There is a distinct model behind the hypothesis of the vicious circle: the growth of income depends on investment; investment depends on saving; saving depends on income. The model pivots on the notion that the low level of income itself prevents the investment required to raise it, hence a zero or negligible rate of economic growth. The model is refuted by obvious reality. If an hypothesis conflicts with empirical evidence, especially if it does so on a massive scale, as in this case, this means that either the variables specified are unimportant or they do not interact in the manner postulated. Both these defects apply in this instance.

The volume of investible funds is not a critical independent determinant of economic advance. If it were, millions of people could not have advanced from poverty to prosperity within a few years.

Much research by leading scholars, including Nobel Laureate Simon Kuznets, has confirmed that capital formation was a minor factor in the progress of the West since the eighteenth century, a period particularly congenial to productive investment. And these findings refer to capital formation and not simply to the volume of investible funds.

Poor people can generate or secure sufficient funds to start on the road to progress if they are motivated to improve their material condition and are not inhibited by government policy or lack of public security. They can save modest amounts even from small incomes to make possible direct investment in agriculture, small-scale trading, the purchase of simple tools and equipment, and for many other purposes.

One general feature of the early stages of economic progress is the replacement of subsistence production by market production for wider exchange. This process is accompanied by certain types of capital formation, important categories of which are incompletely recorded in statistics or altogether unrecorded. This applies to the establishment, extension, and improvement of agricultural properties, for instance the planting of cocoa or rubber trees in plantations on small holdings where the output is collected and distributed by traders. These categories of capital formation are indispensable for the advance from subsistence production. They usually do not require monetary savings or investment, which explains why they often escape statistical record. My experiences in West Africa and Southeast Asia, in which I studied the cocoa industry and the rubber industry, have alerted me to the significance of such categories of capital formation.

What has to be remembered and emphasised is that having capital is the result of successful economic performance, not its precondition. Economic performance depends on personal, cultural, and political factors, on people's aptitudes, attitudes, motivations, and social and political institutions.

Where these are favourable, capital will be generated locally or attracted from abroad.

Poverty or riches, personal and social satisfaction depend on people, on their culture, and on their political arrangements. Understand this sequence, and you understand the most important cause of wealth or deprivation.

Governments and enterprises of poor countries have access to commercial external funds. For instance, in black Africa, European merchants routinely lend to their trustworthy African customers, mostly traders. Indeed, this is virtually a condition of doing business there. The traders in turn lend to farmers or to smaller traders. Much the same applies in South and Southeast Asia. And Third World governments can readily borrow abroad, perhaps too readily. It is evident that ability to borrow abroad does not depend on the level of income, but on responsible conduct and the capacity to use funds productively.

If property rights are clearly defined and reasonably protected, external commercial funds are available even in the face of both poverty and pronounced political risk. Since World War II much foreign investment has taken place in Asia and Africa amidst much political uncertainty. It is unwarranted and distasteful condescension to argue that the peoples of Eastern Europe or of the Third World wish or crave for material progress but, unlike the West, cannot achieve it without donations from abroad.

Development aid is thus clearly not necessary to rescue poor societies from a vicious circle of poverty. Indeed, it is far more likely to keep them in that state. It promotes dependence on others. It encourages the idea that emergence from poverty depends on external donations rather than on people's own efforts, motivation, arrangements, and institutions.

It is official development aid that can create a vicious circle. Poverty is instanced as ground for aid; aid creates dependence and thus keeps people in poverty.

Nor are such external subventions sufficient for economic advance. The many billions of dollars of official aid over the years to Ethiopia, Sudan, and many other African countries have not secured their progress. The massive inflow of gold and silver from Latin America to Spain in the sixteenth and seventeenth centuries also failed to promote economic advance in that country.

I may in passing briefly note two arguments related to the notion of the vicious circle. One is that the poverty of Third World countries inhibits government spending on education, which is deemed necessary to raise incomes. However, aid-recipient governments spend lavishly on prestige projects and on armaments while neglecting education. For instance, under the Indian Second Five Year Plan (1956–1961) expenditure on elementary education was about one-half of the cost of each of three steel plants in the public sector. This occurs in a country where four-fifths of the adults were illiterate, and about one-third of elementary school teachers were completely untrained, and there were not even rudimentary schools for most of the children.

This offshoot of the vicious circle argument also leaves open such questions as the relation between formal schooling and economic advance both generally and under the conditions of Third World countries. According to the second argument related to the vicious circle, the poverty of Third World governments precludes a sufficient scale of programmes for population control. This offshoot of the vicious circle is again insubstantial. People in the Third World are generally, though not invariably, well aware of both traditional and modern forms of contraception. The great majority of children born in the Third World are wanted by their parents (at any rate by their fathers). Moreover, material achievement and progress do not depend on capital and land per head, but, as I have already mentioned, on personal, cultural, and political factors, on people's aptitudes, attitudes, motivations, and social and political institutions. In other words, economic achievement and advance depend on people's conduct not on their numbers.

The notion of the vicious circle also reflects unwarranted condescension. It has been known since at least Hobbes's *Leviathan* that in charitable donations the dispenser of the donation derives at least as much satisfaction as the recipient. The vicious circle argument implies that while the West was able to advance without external donations, the peoples of the Third World, while craving for material progress, cannot attain it without donations from the West. This makes us feel superior even when we beat our breasts for alleged damage the West is said to have inflicted on poor countries.

WHAT CAN SUBSIDIES ACHIEVE?

External donations are thus evidently neither necessary nor sufficient for the emergence from poverty of poor countries. This still leaves open the question whether they promote or retard economic advance. It may seem self-evident that they must be helpful to advance. As they represent an inflow of subsidised resources, it may appear that they must improve economic conditions and prospects; however, this does not follow. The inflow of subsidies sets up various adverse repercussions which can far outweigh any benefits and are indeed likely to do so.

To begin with a technical point: external subsidies raise the real rate of exchange in the receiving country and thereby impair foreign trade competitiveness. This effect can be offset to the extent that the subsidies enhance the overall productivity of resources, which is the usual result of an inflow of private capital, especially equity capital expected to yield a commercial return. But such an increase in productivity is much less likely with official subsidies, as these are rarely expected to produce a positive real return. Furthermore, any increase in productivity can occur only after a time lag of years over which the higher real exchange rate makes for continued dependence on external assistance.

Subventions from abroad promote or reinforce the belief that economic improvement depends on outside forces. The prospect of subsidies encourages governments to seek economic improvement through beggary or blackmail from external sources rather than to consider the potentialities of change at home.

Unlike manna from heaven, which descends indiscriminately on the whole population, these subsidies go to governments. In some instances, subsidies go through governments rather than to them. In our context the distinction is immaterial because the direction and use of the funds require government approval in the recipient countries. They therefore increase the resources, patronage, and power of the government (that is, the rulers), compared to the rest of society. External subsidies have often helped to sustain governments whose policies have proved so damaging that only the subsidies have enabled them to remain in power and continue with such destructive policies. Altogether, the subsidies have contributed significantly to the disastrous politicisation of life in the Third World since World War II.

When economic or social life is extensively politicised people's fortunes come to depend on government policy and administrative decisions. The stakes, both gains and losses, in the struggle for power, increase greatly. These circumstances encourage or even force people to divert attention, energy, and resources from productive economic activity to concern with the outcome of political and administrative decisions; and the deployment of people's energy and resources necessarily affects the economic performance of any society.

The subsidies also make it easier for governments to restrict the inflow of foreign commercial capital. Inflow of equity capital, together with the commercial, administrative, and technical skills that accompany it, has been a prime instrument of the economic advance of many LDCs. The restrictions are correspondingly damaging.

In recent years the adverse effects of these intergovernmental subsidies have been compounded by preferential treatment of governments trying to promote birth control in the recipient countries. This preferential treatment is based on a misconception that population growth is a major factor behind Third World poverty. In reality poverty in the Third World is not caused by population pressures. Economic achievement and progress depend on people's conduct not their numbers.

Robert MacNamara, former president of the World Bank, has been a leading exponent of the view that population growth is disastrous in the Third World. This is what he has written on this subject: "The greatest single obstacle to the economic and social advancement of the majority of peoples in the undeveloped world is rampant population growth. . . . The threat of unmanageable population pressures is very much like the threat of nuclear war."

The obsession with numbers in this context is misdirected. Some of the poorest countries—for instance, Ethiopia, Uganda, and Zaire—are very sparsely populated. In these countries much of the land is a free good. Conversely some of the most densely populated Third World countries are highly prosperous—witness Hong Kong, Singapore, and Malaysia. These instances confirm the central argument of Professor Julian Simon's book *The Ultimate Resource*, namely that the decisive element in achievement and progress is human conduct.

A DOUBLE ASYMMETRY

It is evident that external subsidies are neither necessary nor sufficient for economic advance. Whether they promote or inhibit it cannot be established conclusively. They are much more likely to retard it.

As commercial capital from abroad is available to these people who can use it productively, it follows that the maximum contribution of external subsidies to economic advance cannot exceed the avoided cost of borrowing, that is interest and amortisation charges as proportion of national income which would have been payable to the lenders. The most the subsidies can do is to reduce the cost of a resource that is not a major independent factor in economic advance. Except possibly for very small economies, this benefit is far too small to affect the national income appreciably.

In its effects on economic advance there is a double asymmetry in the operation of aid. The first asymmetry is the following. Any favourable effect through the reduction in the cost of investible resources is a saving in the cost of a resource that is not critical for development. Major adverse effects, on the other hand, operate on critical determinants, namely political and social determinants, and to some extent also on international competitiveness.

The second asymmetry is that a volume of subsidies which is too small to benefit economic performance appreciably, is nevertheless amply sufficient to bring about adverse effects. It is the relationship of the subsidies to national income which is relevant to the favourable effect, namely a reduction in the cost of investible funds. And because subsidies go to governments, it is the relationship of the subsidies to government receipts and foreign exchange earnings that is relevant to major adverse repercussions. Because national income is necessarily a large multiple of tax receipts and foreign exchange earnings, the subsidies are necessarily far larger relative to tax receipts and foreign exchange earnings than they are to national income.

AID AND POVERTY

The argument for aid most widely canvassed since the early 1980s has been that it improves the lot of the poorest in LDCs. But the subsidies do not go to the pathetic figures pictured in aid propaganda. They go to their rulers, who are often directly responsible for the hardship of their subjects. Even when this is not so, it is still the case that the condition of the poorest is very low among the priorities of aid recipients, as is evident from their policies, including the patterns of government spending.

Over most of the Third World there is no machinery for state relief of acute poverty and need. Thus, even if a recipient government wanted to use aid to help the poorest, this can be difficult, even impossible. What is more important, such help may not accord with the political or personal interests or ideological priorities of the Third World rulers, or indeed with local mores. In fact, it often conflicts with these priorities. This situation is evident in multiracial, multitribal, or multicultural countries. Examples include Sudan and Sri Lanka. The Singhalese-dominated government in Sri Lanka will not use resources to help the poorest among the Tamil population. Nor is the Moslem-dominated government of the Sudan likely to help the poorest among the Christian and animist population in the south of that country.

In many aid recipient countries it is the poorest who are worst hit by policies such as enforced population transfers, suppression of trade, forced collectivisation, and also by the civil wars and other forms of breakdown of public security. These policies and conditions have forced large numbers of people to rely for their existence on precarious subsistence production, the hazards of which have become particularly plain in Africa.

Indeed, as we have seen, the criterion of the allocation of much Western aid does nothing to discourage policies of impoverishment or immiseration and is in fact more likely to reward them. Thus, the more damaging the policies, the more acute becomes the need, the more effective become appeals for aid. The experience of Ethiopia and the Sudan in the 1980s makes this clear. The destructive policies of these governments have been largely responsible for the mass misery which in turn has been so effective in eliciting large sums of both official aid and private charity.

Although government-to-government subsidies can do little or nothing either for economic development or for relief of the worst poverty, they can alleviate acute shortages, especially of imports. By maintaining a minimum level of consumption, the subsidies avert total collapse and conceal from the population, at least temporarily, the worst effects of destructive policies. These subsidies also suggest external endorsement of damaging policies. These results in turn help the government to remain in power and to persist in these policies without provoking popular revolt.

This role of external subsidies in alleviating an acute shortage of consumer goods is pertinent to the extension of this policy to postcommunist governments. Reformist postcommunist governments face formidable obstacles resulting from legacies of totalitarian command economies. Attempted reforms engender popular discontent exacerbated by shortage of consumer goods including necessities. In such conditions subsidies for a strictly limited period and directly linked to reformist policies may be helpful or even necessary for the survival of the reformers. This in turn may serve the humanitarian and political interest of Western donors.

REFORM OF AID

These official government-to-government subsidies ought to be terminated or at least drastically curtailed. This seems impractical, partly because of the momentum of existing commitments, partly because of the extremely powerful and articulate interest groups behind the policy. But there are certain reforms that, if implemented, could bring the operation of these transfers closer to their proclaimed objectives.

The most important single reform would be a radical change in the criteria of allocation. These subsidies should go to those governments whose policies are most likely to promote the economic progress and general welfare of their peoples through humane leadership, effective administration, and the extension of personal freedom. Such a reform would remove the most conspicuous anomalies of official aid and enable it to make whatever contribution it can to improve the condition and prospects of the poorest.

This proposal differs altogether from suggestions to link further aid to the adoption of more market-oriented policies by the recipients. Such suggestions are unlikely to be implemented in practice. Extensive state control implies concentration of power, the exercise of patronage, and conferment of privileges. Such a situation suits the purposes of most aid-recipient governments. They are likely to abandon it only if its continued pursuit would threaten an economic breakdown endangering their position. Otherwise, they are unlikely to do more than pay lip service to the market, combined perhaps with some changes in macroeconomic financial policies (including foreign exchange policies) and some largely cosmetic changes in other directions.

To subsidise governments before they have clearly abandoned policies that suit their interests, makes it easier for them to continue existing policies. As U.S. Senator Strom Thurmond has said, "you cannot get a hog to butcher itself."

Official subsidies should be bilateral, not multilateral. This would permit some minimal control by the elected representatives of the taxpayers who are the real donors. Moreover, under the bilateral system there is somewhat closer contact between the suppliers and the users of the funds, which promotes their more effective use. It is also easier to discontinue bilateral subsidies in the face of patently destructive and barbarous policies.

To serve the proclaimed purposes of foreign aid, the subsidies ought to be "untied" (that is, separated from purchases of exports from particular donors). Subsidies to Third World governments could then be distinguished from support of exporters and their bankers in the donor countries.

Aid ought to take the form of straightforward grants rather than subsidised loans. Such loans confuse donations with investment and set up tensions between donors and recipients. Moreover, when tied aid and subsidised loans are linked, as they often are in practice, it becomes quite impossible to ascertain who gets how much and from whom; that is, whether and to what extent the taxpayers of the donor countries subsidise the aid-recipient governments, rather than various interests in their own countries.

Such proposals for reform may be worth reciting, but they are unlikely to be implemented. Both the policy of foreign aid and its methods and practices suit the purposes of powerful interests, especially the official international organisations and exporters of goods and services in the donor countries.

Unless there is overwhelming pressure to the contrary, there is therefore little prospect in the foreseeable future of substantial reform of the procedures and practices of official aid, including the methods of allocation. These are likely to persist in the extension of subsidies to the governments of Eastern Europe and Russia.

Western Guilt and Third World Poverty

Come, fix upon me that accusing eye.
I thirst for accusation.

W. B. Yeats

1

Yeats's words might indeed have been written to describe the wide, even welcome, acceptance by the West of the accusation that it is responsible for the poverty of the Third World (i.e., most of Asia, Africa, and Latin America).[1] Western responsibility for Third World backwardness is a persistent theme of the United Nations and its many affiliates.[2] It has been welcomed by spokesmen of the Third World and of the Communist bloc, notably so at international gatherings where it is often endorsed by official representatives of the West, especially the United States. It is also widely canvassed in the universities, the churches, and the media the world over.

Acceptance of emphatic routine allegations that the West is responsible for Third World poverty reflects and reinforces Western feelings of guilt. It has enfeebled Western diplomacy, both towards the ideologically much more aggressive Soviet bloc and also towards the Third World. And the West has come to abase itself before countries with negligible resources and no real power. Yet the allegations can be shown to be without foundation. They are readily accepted because the Western public has little first-hand knowledge of the Third World and because of widespread feelings of guilt. The West has never had it so good and has never felt so bad about it.

2

A few characteristic examples will illustrate the general theme of Western responsibility. To begin with academics. The late Paul A. Baran, professor of

This essay originally appeared in *Commentary Magazine* 61, 1 January 1976.

[1] In current usage the Third World means most of Asia except Japan and Israel, most of Africa except white southern Africa, and Latin America. Classification of the oil-producing countries is often vague—sometimes they are included in the Third World, sometimes not.

[2] Throughout this chapter, Western responsibility refers to the accusation that the West has inflicted backwardness or poverty on the Third World. This usage again accords with standard practice. The different question of moral responsibility for the relief of poverty is examined in Chapter VII.

economics at Stanford, was a highly regarded development economist. He was a prominent and influential exponent of Western guilt in the early days of contemporary development economics. He contributed the chapter on economic development to the *Survey of Contemporary Economics* published by the American Economic Association, and his book *The Political Economy of Growth* is a widely prescribed university textbook. In it Baran wrote:

> To the dead weight of stagnation characteristic of pre-industrial society was added the entire restrictive impact of monopoly capitalism. The economic surplus appropriated in lavish amounts by monopolistic concerns in backward countries is not employed for productive purposes. It is neither plowed back into their own enterprises nor does it serve to develop others.[3]

This categorical statement is wholly and obviously untrue because throughout the underdeveloped world large agricultural, mineral, commercial, and industrial complexes have been built up through profits reinvested locally.

Professor Peter Townsend of Essex University is perhaps the most prominent British academic writer on poverty. In his book, *The Concept of Poverty,* he wrote:

> I argued that the poverty of deprived nations is comprehensible only if we attribute it substantially to the existence of a system of international social stratification, a hierarchy of societies with vastly different resources in which the wealth of some is linked historically and contemporaneously to the poverty of others. This system operated crudely in the era of colonial domination, and continues to operate today, though more subtly, through systems of trade, education, political relations, military alliances, and industrial corporations.[4]

This again cannot be so. The poorest and most backward countries have until recently had no external economic contacts and often have never been Western colonies. It is therefore obvious that their backwardness cannot be explained by colonial domination or international social stratification. And there are no industrial corporations in the least developed countries of the Third World (the so-called Fourth World) such as Afghanistan, Chad, Bhutan, Burundi, Nepal, and Sikkim.

In this realm of discourse university students echo what they have learnt from their mentors. About ten years ago a student group at Cambridge published a pamphlet on the subject of the moral obligations of the West to the Third World. The following was its key passage:

> We took the rubber from Malaya, the tea from India, raw materials from all over the world and gave almost nothing in return.

[3] Paul A. Baran, *The Political Economy of Growth* (New York: Monthly Review Press, 1957), p. 177.

[4] Peter Townsend, *The Concept of Poverty* (London: Heinemann, 1970), pp. 41–42.

This is as nearly the opposite of the truth as one can find. The British took the rubber *to* Malaya and the tea *to* India. There were no rubber trees in Malaya or anywhere in Asia (as suggested by their botanical name, *Hevea braziliensis*) until about one hundred years ago, when the British took the first rubber seeds there out of the Amazon jungle. From these sprang the huge rubber industry—now very largely Asian-owned. Tea plants were brought to India by the British somewhat earlier; their origin is shown in the botanical name *Camilla sinensis*, as well as in the phrase "all the tea in China."

Charles Clarke, a former president of the National Union of Students, said in his presidential address delivered in December 1976: "For over a hundred years British industry has been draining wealth away from those countries." Far from draining wealth from the less developed countries, British industry helped to create it there, as external commerce promoted economic advance in large areas of the Third World where there was no wealth to be drained.

Western churches and charities are on the same bandwagon. Professor Ronald J. Sider is a prominent American churchman. In an article entitled "How We Oppress the Poor" in *Christianity Today* (16 July 1976), an influential Evangelical magazine, he wrote about the "stranglehold which the developed West has kept on the economic throats of the Third World" and then went on to say, "It would be wrong to suggest that 210 million Americans bear sole responsibility for all the hunger and injustice in today's world. All the rich developed countries are directly involved. . . . We are participants in a system that dooms even more people to agony and death than the slave system did." These are evident fantasies. Famines occur in Third World countries largely isolated from the West. So far from condemning Third World people to death, Western contacts have been behind the large increase in life expectation in the Third World, so often deplored as the population explosion by the same critics.

Many charities have come to think it advantageous to play on the theme of Western responsibility. According to a widely publicized Oxfam advertisement of 1972:

> Coffee is grown in poor developing countries like Brazil, Colombia and Uganda. But that does not stop rich countries like Britain exploiting their economic weakness by paying as little for their raw coffee as we can get away with. On top of this, we keep charging more and more for the manufactured goods they need to buy from us. So? We get richer at their expense. Business is Business.

A similar advertisement was run about cocoa. Both advertisements were subsequently dropped in the face of protests by actual and potential subscribers. The allegations in these advertisements are largely meaningless, and they are also unrelated to reality. The world prices of coffee and cocoa, which were as it happens very high in the 1970s, are determined by market forces and not prescribed by the West. On the other hand, the farmers in many of the exporting countries receive far less than the market prices because they are subject to very high export taxes and similar government levies. The insistence on the allegedly low prices paid by the West to the producers and the lack of any reference to the penal taxation of the producers locally are examples that this guilt literature is concerned more with the flagellation of the West than with improving the conditions of the local population.

The intellectuals outside the academies and churches are also well to the fore. Cyril Connolly wrote in an article entitled "Black Man's Burden" (*Sunday Times,* London, 23 February 1969):

> It is a wonder that the white man is not more thoroughly detested than he is. . . . In our dealings with every single country, greed, masked by hypocrisy, led to unscrupulous coercion of the native inhabitants. . . . Cruelty, greed and arrogance . . . characterized what can be summed up in one word, exploitation.

If this were true, Third World countries would now be poorer than they were before Western contacts. In fact, they are generally much better off.

Insistence that the West has caused Third World poverty is collective self-accusation. The notion itself originated in the West. For instance, Marxism is a Western ideology, as is the belief that economic differences are anomalous and unjust and that they reflect exploitation. But people in the Third World, especially articulate people with contacts with the West, readily believed what they were told by prominent academics and other intellectuals, the more so because the idea accorded with their interests and inclinations.

Inspired by the West, Third World politicians have come habitually to insist that the West has exploited and still exploits their countries. Dr. Nkrumah, a major Third World figure of the 1950s and 1960s, was a well-known exponent of this view. He described Western capitalism as "a world system of financial enslavement and colonial oppression and exploitation of a vast majority of the population of the earth by a handful of the so-called civilized nations."[5] In fact, until the advent of Dr. Nkrumah, Ghana (the former Gold Coast) was a prosperous country as a result of cocoa exports to the West, with the cocoa farmers the most prosperous and the subsistence producers the poorest groups there.

Julius Nyerere, president of Tanzania, is a highly regarded, almost venerated, world figure.[6] He said in the course of a state visit to London in 1975: "If the rich nations go on getting richer and richer at the expense of the poor, the poor of the world must demand a change." When the

[5] Kwame Nkrumah, *Towards Colonial Freedom* (London: Heinemann, 1962). Cf. also P. T. Bauer, *Dissent on Development* (Cambridge: Harvard University Press, 1972), chaps. 3 and 4.

[6] An adulatory profile in *The Observer* (23 November 1975) cosily referred to Nyerere as "St. Julius." An article in the *Financial Times* (11 August 1975) described him as "Africa's senior statesman and a man of formidable intellect."

West established substantial contact with Tanganyika (effectively the present Tanzania) in the nineteenth century, this was an empty region, thinly populated with tribal people exposed to Arab slavers. Its relatively modest progress since then has been the work primarily of Asians and Europeans.

The notion of Western exploitation of the Third World is standard in publications and statements emanating from the Soviet Union and other communist countries. Here is one example. The late Soviet academician Potekhin was a prominent Soviet authority on Africa. He is worth quoting because Soviet economic writings are taken seriously in Western universities:

> Why is there little capital in Africa? The reply is evident. A considerable part of the national income which is supposed to make up the accumulation fund and to serve as the material basis of progress is exported outside Africa without any equivalent.[7]

No funds are exported from the poorest parts of Africa. Such remittances as there are from the more prosperous parts of the continent (generally very modest in the case of Black Africa, to which Potekhin refers) are partial returns on the resources supplied. In the most backward areas there are no foreigners and no foreign capital: It is the opposite of the truth to say that the reason there is little capital in Africa is that much of the national income is "exported . . . without any equivalent." In Africa as elsewhere in the Third World, the most prosperous areas are those with most commercial contacts with the West.

I could cite many more such allegations, but the foregoing should suffice to illustrate the general theme. In subsequent sections I shall note more specific allegations, some of them even more virulent than those already quoted.

3

Far from the West having caused the poverty in the Third World, contact with the West has been the principal agent of material progress there. The materially more advanced societies and regions of the Third World are those with which the West established the most numerous, diversified, and extensive contacts: the cash-crop producing areas and entrepôt ports of Southeast Asia, West Africa, and Latin America; the mineral-producing areas of Africa and the Middle East; and cities and ports throughout Asia, Africa, the Caribbean, and Latin America. The level of material achieve-

---

[7] I. Potekhin, *Problems of Economic Independence of African Countries* (Moscow: Academy of Sciences, 1962), pp. 14–15.

ment usually diminishes as one moves away from the foci of Western impact. The poorest and most backward people have few or no external contacts; witness the aborigines, pygmies, and desert peoples.

All this is neither new nor surprising since the spread of material progress from more to less advanced regions is a commonplace of history. In medieval Europe, for instance, the more advanced regions of Central and Eastern Europe and Scandinavia were the areas with the most contacts with France, the Low Countries, and Italy, the most advanced parts of Europe at the time. The West was materially far ahead of the present Third World countries when it established extensive and diverse economic contacts with them in the nineteenth and twentieth centuries. It was through these contacts that human and material resources, skills, capital, and new ideas, including the idea of material progress itself (and, incidentally, that of Western guilt too) flowed from the West to the Third World.

In recent times the role of external contacts in promoting economic advance in the Third World has been much more significant than that of similar contacts in the earlier history of Europe. To begin with, and as just noted, the very idea of material progress in the sense of sustained, steady, and increasing control over man's environment is a Western concept. People in the Third World did not think of these terms before the advent of Western man. Scholars of such widely differing philosophical and political persuasion as, for instance, J. B. Bury and Christopher Dawson, have for long recognized the Western origin of the idea of material progress. The Western impulse behind economic advance in the Third World has also been acknowledged by writers who recognized this progress but warned against the disturbing, even corrosive, results of the sudden impact of contact with materially much more advanced societies.[8]

The West developed multifarious contacts with the Third World in the nineteenth and twentieth centuries, when the difference in economic attainment between the West and these regions was very wide, much wider than such differences had been in the past. Thus these contacts offered correspondingly greater opportunities, especially in view of the great improvements in transport and communications over the last two hundred years or so.

Since the middle of the nineteenth century, commercial contacts established by the West have improved material conditions out of all recognition over much of the Third World, notably in Southeast Asia; parts of the Middle East; much of Africa, especially West Africa and parts of East and Southern Africa; and very large parts of Latin America, including Mexico, Guatemala, Venezuela, Colombia, Peru, Chile, Brazil, Uruguay, and Argentina. The transformation of Malaya (the present Malaysia) is instruc-

[8] A list of such warnings and objections will be found in Bauer, *Dissent on Development.*

tive. In the 1890s it was a sparsely populated area of Malay hamlets and fishing villages. By the 1930s it had become the hub of the world's rubber and tin industries. By then there were large cities and excellent communications in a country where millions of Malays, Chinese, and Indians now lived much longer and better than they had formerly, either in their countries of origin or in Malaya.

Large parts of West Africa were also transformed over roughly the same period as a result of Western contacts. Before 1890 there was no cocoa production in the Gold Coast or Nigeria, only very small production of cotton and groundnuts, and small exports of palm oil and palm kernels. By the 1950s all these had become staples of world trade. They were produced by Africans on African-owned properties. But this was originally made possible by Westerners who established public security and introduced modern methods of transport and communications. Over this period imports both of capital goods and of mass consumer goods for African use also rose from insignificant amounts to huge volumes. The changes were reflected in government revenues, literacy rates, school attendance, public health, life expectation, infant mortality, and many other indicators.

Statistics by themselves can hardly convey the far-reaching transformation which took place over this period in West Africa and elsewhere in the Third World. In West Africa, for instance, slave trading and slavery were still widespread at the end of the nineteenth century. They had practically disappeared by the end of World War I. Many of the worst endemic and epidemic diseases for which West Africa was notorious throughout the nineteenth century had disappeared by World War II. External contacts also brought about similar far-reaching changes over much of Latin America.

The role of Western contacts in the material progress of Black Africa deserves further notice. As late as the second half of the nineteenth century Black Africa was without even the simplest, most basic ingredients of modern social and economic life. These were brought there by Westerners over the last hundred years or so. This is true of such fundamentals as public security and law and order; wheeled traffic (Black Africa never invented the wheel) and mechanical transport (before the arrival of Westerners, transport in Black Africa was almost entirely by human muscle); roads, railways, and manmade ports; the application of science and technology to economic activity; towns with substantial buildings, clean water, and sewerage facilities; public health care, hospitals, and the control of endemic and epidemic diseases; formal education. These advances resulted from peaceful commercial contacts. These contacts also made easier the elimination of the Atlantic slave trade, the virtual elimination of the slave trade from Africa to the Middle East, and even the elimination of slavery within Africa.

Although peaceful commercial contacts had nothing to do with the Atlantic slave trade, in the contemporary climate it is impossible not to refer to that trade in a discussion of Western responsibility for Third World poverty. Horrible and destructive as was the Atlantic slave trade, it cannot be claimed legitimately as a cause of African backwardness, still less of Third World poverty. Asia was altogether untouched by it. The most backward parts of Africa, such as the interior of Central and Southern Africa and most of East Africa, were largely unaffected by it.[9]

The slave trade between Africa and the Middle East antedated the Atlantic slave trade by centuries and far outlasted it. Slavery was endemic over much of Africa long before the emergence of the Atlantic slave trade, and it was eventually stamped out by the West. Arabs and Africans do not seem to feel guilty about slavery and the slave trade; but Western Europeans and Americans often do and are made to do so. And yet it was due to their efforts that these practices were largely eliminated. Guilt is a prerogative of the West.

Western activities—supplemented at times by those of non-Western immigrants, notably Chinese, Indians, and Levantines whose large-scale migration was made possible by Western initiative—have thus transformed material conditions in many parts of the Third World. All this is not to say that over the past hundred years there has been substantial material advance uniformly throughout the Third World. Large areas, especially in the interior of the Third World, have had few contacts with the West. Moreover, in much of the Third World the political, social, and personal determinants of economic performance are often uncongenial to economic achievement. And the policies of many governments plainly obstruct economic achievement and progress. Again, people often refuse to abandon attitudes and mores which obstruct economic performance. They are not prepared to give up their established ways for the sake of greater prosperity. This is a preference which is neither unjustified nor reprehensible.

Such considerations in no way warrant the allegations that Western contacts have obstructed or retarded Third World progress. Wherever local conditions have permitted it, commercial contacts with the West, and generally established by the West, have eliminated the worst diseases, reduced or even eliminated famine, extended life expectations, and improved living standards.

[9] In fact, the areas most involved in the Atlantic slave trade, particularly West Africa, have become the economically most advanced areas in Black Africa. A recent study of precolonial South-Eastern Nigeria examines the economic development promoted by the slave trade which "led to sufficient economic development of the region" to enable the profitable trade in palm oil to burgeon in the early nineteenth century. David Northrup, *Trade Without Rulers: Pre-colonial Economic Development in South-Eastern Nigeria* (Oxford: Clarendon Press, 1978), p. 176.

4

Many of the assertions of Western responsibility for Third World poverty imply that the prosperity of relatively well-to-do persons, groups, and societies is achieved at the expense of the less well-off. These assertions express the misconception that the incomes of the well-to-do have been taken from others. In fact, with a few clearly definable exceptions, which do not apply to the relations between the West and the Third World, incomes whether of the rich or of the poor are earned by their recipients. In the Third World it is an article of faith of the most influential and articulate groups that their societies have been exploited by the West, both by Western individuals and Western companies, and also by locally resident ethnic minorities such as the Chinese in Southeast Asia, Asians in East Africa, and Levantines in West Africa. The appeal of these misconceptions is all too familiar. They are especially useful to politicians who have promised a prosperity which they cannot deliver. But they are also useful to other influential local groups who expect to benefit from policies inspired by these ideas, especially from the expropriation of foreign enterprises or discrimination against minorities.

In recent decades certain readily recognizable influences have reinforced the notion that the prosperity of some group means that others have been exploited. The impact of Marxist-Leninist ideology has been one such influence. In this ideology any return on private capital implies exploitation, and service industries are regarded as unproductive. Thus, earnings of foreign capital and the incomes of foreigners or ethnic minorities in the service industries are evidence of forms of exploitation. Further, neo-Marxist literature has extended the concept of the proletariat to the peoples of the Third World, most of whom are in fact small-scale cultivators. In this literature, moreover, a proletariat is exploited by definition and is poor because it is exploited.[10]

The idea of Western responsibility for Third World poverty has also been promoted by the belief in a universal basic equality of people's economic capacities and motivations. This belief is closely related to egalitarian ideology and policy which have experienced a great upsurge in recent decades. If people's attributes and motivations are the same everywhere and yet some societies are richer than others, this suggests that the former have ex-

---

[10] This extension of Marxist-Leninist ideology is reflected, for instance, in the passage from the Soviet Academician Potekhin, section 2 above. Marxist-Leninist statements are apt to be designed for political purposes. Thus, in Potekhin's booklet, the passage I have quoted is followed immediately by the injunction that Western enterprises in Africa should be expropriated and economic activity collectivized. This injunction is now accepted by a number of African states.

ploited the rest. Because the public in the West has little direct contact with the Third World, it is often easy to put across the idea that Western conduct and policies have caused poverty in the Third World.

The recent practice of referring to the poor as deprived or underprivileged again helps the notion that the rich owe their prosperity to the exploitation of the poor. Yet how could the incomes of, for example, people in Switzerland or North America have been taken from, say, the aborigines of Papua, or the desert peoples or pygmies of Africa? Indeed, who deprived these groups and of what?[11]

5

The principal assumption behind the idea of Western responsibility for Third World poverty is that the prosperity of individuals and societies generally reflects the exploitation of others. Some variants or derivatives of this theme are often heard, usually geared to particular audiences. One of these variants is that colonialism has caused the poverty of Asia and Africa. It has particular appeal in the United States where hostility to colonialism is traditional. For a different and indeed opposite reason, it is at times effective in stirring up guilt in Britain, the foremost former colonial power.

Whatever one thinks of colonialism, it cannot be held responsible for Third World poverty. Some of the most backward countries never were colonies, as for instance Afghanistan, Tibet, Nepal, Liberia. Ethiopia is perhaps an even more telling example (it was an Italian colony for only six years in its long history). Again, many of the Asian and African colonies progressed very rapidly during colonial rule, much more so than the independent countries in the same area. At present one of the few remaining European colonies is Hong Kong—whose prosperity and progress should be familiar.[12] It is plain that colonial rule has not been the cause of Third World poverty.

Nor is the prosperity of the West the result of colonialism. The most advanced and the richest countries never had colonies, including Switzerland and the Scandinavian countries; and some were colonies of others and were already very prosperous as colonies, as for instance North America and Australasia. The prosperity of the West was generated by its own peoples and was not taken from others. The European countries were already materially far ahead of the areas where they established colonies.

In recent years the charges that colonialism causes Third World poverty have been expanded to cover "colonialism in all its forms." The terms "eco-

[11] Underprivileged is a nonsense expression akin to under- or overfed. Privilege connotes special advantages conferred on some people and denied to others.

[12] In 1997 Britain gave over Hong Kong to China.

nomic colonialism" and "neocolonialism" have sprung up to cover external private investment, the activities of multinational companies, and indeed almost any form of economic relationship between relatively rich and relatively poor regions or groups. Reference to "colonialism in all its forms" as a cause of Third World poverty is a major theme at the United Nations Conference on Trade and Development (UNCTAD) meetings. This terminology has become common currency in both academic literature and in the media. It regularly confuses poverty with colonial status, a concept which has normally meant lack of political sovereignty.

One unusually direct formulation of these ideas (which are normally expressed in much more convoluted form in the academic and official literature) was provided in an editorial in the June 1978 issue of *Poverty and Power* published by War on Want, a British charity:

> We see poverty in the Third World as a result of colonial looting in the past and neocolonial exploitation in the present.

The demise of political colonialism has probably been another important factor behind the shift in terminology. Disappearance of colonial rule has forced the accusers of the West to find new ground for their charges. Hence the terminology of neocolonialism and economic colonialism. The usage represents a shift in the basis of accusation and at the same time it retains the benefits of the older, familiar terminology. The influence of Marxist-Leninist doctrine has also promoted the new terminology. According to Marxist-Leninist ideology, colonial status and foreign investment are by definition evidence of exploitation. In fact, foreign private investment and the activities of the multinational companies have expanded opportunities and raised incomes and government revenues in the Third World. Reference to economic colonialism end neocolonialism both debase the language and distort the truth.[13]

6

The West is now widely accused of manipulating international trade to the detriment of the Third World. This accusation is a major theme of the demands for a New International Economic Order. In particular, the West is supposed to inflict unfavourable and persistently deteriorating terms of trade on the Third World. Among other untoward results, this influence is

---

[13] A convenient recent example is a statement by the Ayatollah Khomeini in January 1979: "Our people are weary of it (colonial domination). Following their example other countries will free themselves from the colonial grip." *Daily Telegraph*, 10 January 1979. In its long history Iran never was a Western colony. Further examples of this usage are noted in *Dissent on Development*, chap. 3, "The Economics of Resentment."

said to have resulted in a decline in the share of the Third World in total world trade and also in a large volume of Third World foreign debt. These allegations are again irrelevant, unfounded, and often the opposite of the truth.[14]

The poorest areas of the Third World have no external trade. Their condition shows that the causes of backwardness are domestic and that external commercial contacts are beneficial. Even if the terms of trade were unfavourable on some criterion or other, this would only mean that people do not benefit from foreign trade as much as they would if the terms of trade were more favourable. People benefit from the widening of opportunities which external trade represents. Besides this last and basic conclusion, there are many other objections to the notion that the terms of trade are somehow inherently unfavourable to the Third World, and external commercial contacts damaging to it.

As the Third World comprises most of the world, the aggregation of the terms of trade of all its countries has a very limited meaning. The terms of trade of some Third World countries and groups of countries move differently and often in opposite directions from those of others; the effect of the OPEC price increases on many Third World countries is only one recent and familiar example.

Again, except over very short periods, changes in the terms of trade as conventionally measured are of little welfare significance without reference to changes in the cost of production of exports, the range and quality of imports, and the volume of trade. Insofar as changes in the terms of trade do affect development and welfare, what matters is the amount of imports which can be purchased with a unit of domestic resources. This figure cannot be inferred simply from the ratio of import and export prices because these do not take into account the cost of production of exports. (In technical language, the comparisons relevant to economic welfare and development are the factoral terms of trade, which allow for changes in the cost of production, and not the simple ratio between import and export prices, i.e., crude commodity terms.) Further, expressions such as unfavourable terms of trade are meaningless except by reference to a base period. In recent decades, however, even the crude commodity terms of trade of Third World countries have been exceptionally favourable. When changes in the cost of production, the great improvement in the range and quality of imports, and the huge increase in the volume of trade are taken into account, the external purchasing power of Third World exports is

---

[14] These allegations and the demand for a New International Economic Order are discussed at some length in several essays in Karl Brunner, ed., *The First World and the Third World* (Rochester: University of Rochester Press, 1978). See especially essays by Karl Brunner, Harry G. Johnson, Peter T. Bauer, and Basil S. Yamey.

now relatively high, probably more so than ever before. This situation has made it easier for governments to retain a larger proportion of export earnings through major increases in mining royalty rates, export taxes, and corporation taxes. The imposition of substantial export taxes, often very high in the Third World, makes clear that the terms of trade of a country do not determine people's ability to buy imports, much less their living standards.

The exponents of the idea that the terms of trade of the Third World deteriorate persistently rarely specify the period they envisage for this process. Yet it must come to an end at some stage before the terms of trade decline to zero.[15] Nor is it usually made clear why there should be such a deterioration. It is often implied that the West can somehow manipulate international prices to the disadvantage of the Third World. But the West cannot prescribe international prices. These prices are the outcome of innumerable individual decisions of market participants. They are not prescribed by a single individual decisionmaker, or even by a handful of people acting in collusion.[16]

The share of a country or group of countries in total world trade is by itself no index of prosperity or welfare. Similarly, reduction in this share has by itself no adverse economic implications. It often reflects the expansion of economic activity and trade elsewhere, which does not normally damage but usually benefits those whose relative share has declined. For instance, since the 1950s the large increase in the foreign trade of Japan, the reconstruction of Europe, and the liberalization of intra-European trade have brought about a decline in the share of other groups in world trade, including that of the United States and the United Kingdom. Furthermore, the share of a country or group of countries in world trade is often reduced by domestic developments and in particular by policies unrelated to external circumstances such as increased domestic use of previously exported products, or domestic inflation, or special taxation of exporters, or the intensification of protectionist policies. Merely as an aside, it is worth noting that since World War II the Third World's share of total world trade has in fact much increased compared with earlier times. It is evident that this share has increased hugely under Western influence in the modern period. Before then, the areas forming the present Third World had little external trade. Of course, if international trade harmed the peoples of the Third World as the critics of the West so often allege, then a decline in the

[15] When some ostensible evidence is produced in support of these allegations, it usually turns out to involve shifts in base periods or in the aggregates under discussion. I have examined these matters in some detail in *Dissent on Development,* chap. 6: "A Critique of UNCTAD."

[16] Even if the West had the market power implied in many of these discussions, this would not account for a deterioration of the terms of trade, unless the effectiveness of this power increased persistently. Any such idea would be quite unrelated to reality.

share of the Third World in this trade would be beneficial. Ultimate economic bliss would be attained when the Third World no longer had external economic relations, at any rate with the West.

The external debts of the Third World are not the result or reflection of exploitation. They represent resources supplied. Indeed, much of the current indebtedness of Third World governments consists of soft loans under various aid agreements, frequently supplemented by outright grants. With the worldwide rise in prices, including those of Third World exports, the cost even of these soft loans has diminished greatly. Difficulties of servicing these debts do not reflect external exploitation or unfavourable terms of trade. They are the result of wasteful use of the capital supplied or inappropriate monetary and fiscal policies. Again, the persistent balance of payments deficits of some Third World countries do not mean that they are being exploited or impoverished by the West. Such deficits are inevitable if the government of a country, whether rich or poor, advancing or stagnating, lives beyond its resources and pursues inflationary policies while attempting to maintain overvalued exchange rates. Persistent balance of payments difficulties mean that external resources are being lent to the country over these periods.

The decline of particular economic activities, as for instance the Indian textile industry in the eighteenth century as a result of competition from cheap imports, is habitually instanced as an example of the damage caused to the Third World by trade with the West. This argument identifies the decline of one activity with the decline of the economy as a whole, and the economic interests of one sectional group with those of all members of a society. Cheap imports extend the choice and economic opportunities of people in poor countries. These imports are usually accompanied by the expansion of other activities. If this were not so, the population would be unable to pay for the imports.

The so-called brain drain, the migration of qualified personnel from the Third World to the West, is another allegation of Western responsibility for Third World poverty or stagnation. This is a somewhat more complex issue than those noted so far, but it certainly does not substantiate the familiar accusation. The training of many of the emigrants was financed by the West. Again, formal education is not an indispensable instrument nor even a major instrument of emergence from personal poverty or economic backwardness—witness the rapid progress to prosperity of untrained or even illiterate people in many Third World countries. The enforced exodus or outright expulsion of many enterprising and skilled people from many Third World countries, the maltreatment of ethnic minorities or tribal groups, and the refusal of many Third World governments to allow foreigners to work inhibit development much more than do voluntary departures. And many of these emigrants leave because their own governments cannot or will not use their services. It is not the West nor the emigrants who deprive the society of productive resources: it is these Third World governments.[17]

The West is also said to have damaged the Third World by ethnic discrimination. But the countries in which such discrimination occurred were those where material progress was initiated or promoted by contact with the West. The most backward groups in the Third World (aborigines, desert peoples, nomads, and other tribesfolk) were quite unaffected by ethnic discrimination on the part of Europeans. Many communities against which discrimination was often practised—the Chinese in Southeast Asia, Indians in parts of Southeast Asia, Asians in Africa, and others—have progressed greatly. In any case, discrimination on the basis of colour or race is not a European invention. In much of Africa and Asia and notably in India it has been endemic for many centuries. Finally, any ethnic discrimination by Europeans was negligible compared with the massive and sometimes brutal persecution of ethnic and tribal groups systematically practised by the governments of many independent Asian and African states.

Altogether, it is anomalous or even perverse to suggest that external commercial relations are damaging to development or to the living standards of the people of the Third World. They act as channels for the flow of human and financial resources and for new ideas, methods, and crops. They benefit people by providing a large and diverse source of imports and by opening up markets for exports. Because of the vast expansion of world trade in recent decades and the development of technology in the West, the material advantages from external contacts are now greater than ever before. The suggestion that these relations are detrimental is not only unfounded but also damaging. For instance, it has often served as a specious but plausible justification for official restrictions on the volume or diversity of these relations.

The basic realities of the results of external contacts have been obfuscated by the practise, rife both in public discussion and in the contemporary development literature, of confusing governments or elites with the population at large.[18] Many Third World governments and their local al-

---

[17] An article in *The Observer* (22 July 1979) was entitled "The boat people's 'brain drain' punishes Vietnam." The article suggested that the refugees from Vietnam were selfish and unpatriotic people who left because they could earn more elsewhere and because they would not accept the new socialist order. It suggested further that this brain drain deprived the country of much-needed skills, especially medical skills. The article used the terms *brain drain, exodus,* and *loss* to describe what was in fact a well-documented example of a huge mass expulsion— a revealing misuse of language.

[18] The distinction which applies in many contexts is pertinent also to an assessment of changes in a country's terms of trade. As noted earlier in this section, changes in the terms of trade do not necessarily correspond to the ability of people to buy imports.

lies do indeed often benefit from state economic controls and in particular from the restrictions on external commerce. Such restrictions enable governments to control their subjects more closely, a situation from which the rulers benefit politically and materially. Other articulate and influential local groups also benefit politically and financially from organizing or administering economic controls. These realities are concealed in allegations that the West had forced imports on Third World countries. It is, of course, the rulers who object to the imports desired by their subjects.

The allegations that external trade, and especially imports from the West, are damaging to the populations of the Third World reveal a barely disguised condescension towards the ordinary people there, and even contempt for them. The people, of course, want the imports. If they did not, the imported goods could not be sold. Similarly, the people are prepared to produce for export to pay for these imported goods. To say that these processes are damaging is to argue that people's preferences are of no account in organizing their own lives.

The disparagement of external contacts is relatively recent. Before World War II the role of these contacts as instruments of economic advance was widely recognized in academic and public discussion. Their role in providing both external markets and incentive goods, as well as transforming people's attitudes, was a conspicuous theme of the classical economists, including writers as different in their outlook as Adam Smith, John Stuart Mill, and Karl Marx.

7

Apart from the damage allegedly caused to the Third World by external trade, it is frequently said nowadays that the mere existence and day-to-day activities of the peoples of the West also harm the Third World.

Cheap consumer goods developed and used in the West and available also in the Third World are said to obstruct development there because these goods supposedly encourage spending at the expense of saving. The mainstream development literature calls this the international demonstration effect. This contention disregards the level of consumption and the extension of choice as criteria of development. Yet these matters are what economic development is about. The notion of a damaging international demonstration effect also ignores the role of external contacts as instruments of development. It overlooks the fact that the new consumer goods have to be paid for, which usually requires improved economic performance including such things as more work, additional saving and investment, and readiness to produce for sale instead of for subsistence. Thus this accusation neglects the obvious consideration that a higher and more varied level of consumption is both the principal justification for material progress and an inducement to further economic advance.[19]

An updated version of the international demonstration effect proposes that the eager acceptance of Western consumer goods in the Third World is a form of cultural dependence engendered by Western business. The implication here is that the peoples of the Third World lack the ability to decide for themselves how best to spend their incomes. They are looked on as children, or even as mere puppets manipulated by foreigners at will. In fact, however, Western goods have been accepted selectively and not indiscriminately in the Third World where they have been of massive benefit to millions of people. This charge of cultural dependence is often accompanied by the accusation that the West also damages the Third World through its patent laws. Thus, both the provision of Western goods and also the alleged withholding of them are said to be damaging.

As is not surprising, allegedly lavish consumption habits and the pollution and plunder of the environment in the West have also been pressed into ideological service. A standard formulation is that per capita consumption of food and energy in the United States is many times that in India, so that the American consumer despoils his Indian opposite number on a large scale. Professor Tibor Mende is an influential and widely quoted writer on development. A few years ago he wrote: "According to one estimate, each American has twenty-five times the impact on the environment—as a consumer and polluter—as an Indian" (Newsweek, 23 October 1972). Note the reference to each American as consumer and polluter, but not as a producer.

Even babies are drafted into the campaign to promote Western guilt, notably in the familiar pictures of babies with distended bellies. An article entitled "The Greed of the Super Rich" in the London Sunday Times, 20 August 1978, opens as follows:

> One American baby consumes fifty times more of the world's resources than an Indian baby. . . . The wheat need of the people in Africa's Sahel region could have been met by a twentieth of the wheat European countries use each year to feed cattle.

The West has even come to be accused of mass cannibalism. According to Professor René Dumont, the widely known French agronomist and consultant to international organisations: "in over-consuming meat, which

[19] At the official level, a damaging international demonstration effect may indeed operate by encouraging show projects and unsuitable technologies financed with public funds. But this is not usually what the exponents of the international demonstration effect have in mind. Nor is it appropriate to blame the West for the policies of Third World governments in their adoption of unsuitable external models.

wasted the cereals which could have saved them, we ate the little children of Sahel, of Ethiopia, and of Bangladesh."[20] This grotesque allegation has come to be widely echoed in the West. According to Miss Jill Tweedie of *The Guardian* (London): "A quarter of the world's population lives, quite literally, by killing the other three-quarters" (*The Guardian,* 3 January 1977). And another article prominently featured in *The Guardian* of 11 June 1979 referred to the

> social cannibalism which has reduced over three-quarters of mankind to beggary, poverty and death, not because they don't work, but because their wealth goes to feed, clothe, and shelter a few idle classes in America, Europe, and Japan . . . moneymongers in London and New York and in other Western seats of barons living on profit snatched from the peasants and workers of the world.[21]

Such ridiculous statements could be multiplied many times over. Their expression by prominent academics and by journalists in the so-called quality press tells much about the contemporary intellectual scene.

The West has not caused the famines in the Third World. These have occurred in backward regions with practically no external commerce. The absence of external trading links is often one aspect of the backwardness of these regions. At times it reflects the policies of the rulers who are hostile to traders, especially to nonindigenous traders, and often even to private property. As a matter of interest, it has proved difficult to get emergency supplies to some of the Sahelian areas because of poor communications and official apathy or hostility. Attempts permanently to support the populations of such backward areas with Western official donations would inhibit the development of viable agriculture there.

Contrary to the various allegations and accusations noted in this section, the higher level of consumption in the West is not achieved by depriving others of what they have produced. Western consumption is more than paid for by Western production. This production not only finances domestic consumption but also provides the capital for domestic and foreign investment as well as foreign aid. Thus the gap between production in the West and in the Third World is even greater than the gap in consumption.

8

The West has indeed contributed to Third World poverty, in two senses. These, however, differ radically from the familiar assertions.

---

[20] Quoted by Daniel P. Moynihan, "The United States in Opposition." *Commentary* (March 1975).

[21] The article, written by Ngugi wa Thiang 'O, opened a special survey of Kenya.

First, Western activities since World War II have done much to politicize economic life in the Third World. In the terminal years of British colonial rule the traditional policy of relatively limited government was abandoned in favour of close official economic controls. As a result of this change in policy in most British colonies outside the Far East and Southeast Asia, a readymade framework for state-controlled economies or even for totalitarian states was presented to the incoming independent governments. The operation of official Western aid to Third World governments, reinforced by certain strands in its advocacy and by the criteria of its allocation, has also served to politicize life in the Third World. These controls have wasted resources, restricted social and economic mobility, and also external contacts. They have also provoked fierce political and social strife. These consequences in turn have brought about poverty and even large-scale suffering.

Many independent Third World governments would presumably have attempted in any case to politicize their economies extensively because this greatly enhances the power of the rulers. But they are unlikely to have gone so far as they have in recent years or to have succeeded in their attempts, without Western influence and assistance. But all this does not validate the position of the exponents of Western guilt. The most vocal and influential critics both of colonial rule and of Western contacts with the Third World have emphatically urged large-scale economic controls and other forms of politicization of life in the Third World. Indeed, they have blamed colonial governments and Western influence for not promoting such policies sooner and more vigorously.

Second, Western contacts with the Third World have helped bring about the sharp decline in mortality in the Third World which is behind the recent rapid population growth there. These Western contacts have therefore enabled many more poor people to survive and have thus increased apparent poverty. But this outcome represents an improvement in the condition of people, and is not the result of deprivation.

9

The allegations that external contacts damage the Third World are plainly condescending. They clearly imply that Third World people do not know what is good for them nor even what they want. The image of the Third World as a uniform stagnant mass devoid of distinctive character is another aspect of this condescension. It reflects a stereotype which denies identity, character, personality, and responsibility to the individuals and societies of the Third World. Because the Third World is defined as the whole world with the exception of the West and a handful of Westernised societies (such as Japan and South Africa) it is regarded as if it were all much of a muchness. Time and again the guilt merchants envisage the Third World as an undifferentiated, passive entity, helplessly at the mercy of its environment and of the powerful West.

The exponents of Western guilt further patronize the Third World by suggesting that its economic fortunes past, present, and prospective, are determined by the West; that past exploitation by the West explains Third World backwardness; that manipulation of international trade by the West and other forms of Western misconduct account for persistent poverty; that the economic future of the Third World depends largely on Western donations. According to this set of ideas, whatever happens to the Third World is largely our doing. Such ideas make us feel superior even while we beat our breasts.

A curious mixture of guilt and condescension is also discernible behind the toleration or even support of inhuman policies of many Third World governments. The brutalities of the rulers are often excused on the ostensible ground that they are only following examples set by the West. For instance, when Asian or African governments massively persecute ethnic minorities, they are excused by their Western sympathizers as doing no more than adopting a local variant of ethnic discrimination by Europeans. Similarly, the most offensive and baseless utterances of Third World spokesmen need not be taken seriously because they are only Third World statements, a licence which has been extended to their supporters in the West. In this general scheme of things, neither Third World rulers nor their peoples have minds or wills of their own: they are envisaged as creatures moulded by the West or, at best, as being at the mercy of their own environment. Moreover, like children, they are not altogether responsible for what they do. In any case, we must support them to atone for alleged wrongs which our supposed ancestors may have perpetrated on their supposed ancestors. And economic aid is also necessary to help these children grow up.

Insistence on Western foreign aid is a major theme of the recent literature of Western guilt. But whether or not linked to patronization (and it usually is so linked), the idea of Western guilt is not only unfounded but is also a singularly inappropriate basis for aid. It leads to a disregard of the effects of aid in the recipient countries and of the conduct of the recipient governments. It discourages even cursory examination of the likely political, social, and economic results of Western alms. The prime concern is with divesting the West of resources, not with the effects of its donations.

A feeling of guilt has nothing to do with a sense of responsibility or a sense of compassion. Exponents of guilt are concerned with their own emotional state and that of their fellow citizens, and not with the results of the policies inspired by such sentiments. These policies damage the West. They damage the ordinary people in the Third World even more.

The Liberal Death Wish

You taught me language; and my profit on't
Is, I know how to curse: the red plague rid you.
For learning me your language!

Shakespeare, The Tempest

1

Liberals, Malcolm Bradbury wrote in *Stepping Westward,* are people who embrace their destroyers. Professor Mazrui's 1979 Reith Lectures confirm this perceptive observation.[1] Formerly at Makerere, Professor Mazrui is now professor of political science at the University of Michigan, a prominent liberal institution. As he himself recounts (p. 16), as a youngster he was taken up and helped by Europeans in East Africa. He was educated in Western-organized and -financed institutions in East Africa, Britain, and the United States. Yet hostility to the West pervades the lectures and provides their unifying theme. His view of the recent past is this:

The Berlin Congress opened in 1884 to help seal the fate of the continent for at least another century. The nightmare of European penetration and colonization of Africa was now truly underway. (p. 32)

His vision of the future:

The decline of Western civilization might well be at hand. It is in the interest of humanity that such a decline should take place, allowing the different segments of the human race to enjoy a more equitable share not only of the resources of the planet but also of the capacity to control the march of history. (pp. 86–87)

These assessments explain his proposals for policy, which, as we shall see, are not designed to assist ordinary Africans but to diminish or undermine the West.

In each lecture Professor Mazrui addresses himself to what he considers a paradox. Africa, the first habitat of man, has decayed through human

---

This essay originally appeared in *Encounter* 54, no. 6 (June 1980): 69.

[1] *The African Condition* (The Reith Lectures. London: Heinemann Educational Books, 1980).

neglect; it is now the least habitable continent because of disease, lack of communications and political instability. Africans, though they have not experienced a holocaust such as that experienced by the Jews, or genocide such as that of the indigenous American Indians or Australians at the hands of white people, have been the most humiliated people in history through the slave trade, colonialism and racial discrimination. African societies are not the closest culturally to the West, yet they have recently been rapidly Westernized. In Africa, immense mineral wealth and agricultural potential coexist with extremely low living standards. Africa, the second largest continent, is the most fragmented, split into more than fifty nations, many of them tiny. Finally, Africa, a large continent centrally and strategically located in the world, plays only a marginal role in world affairs.

The causes of the predicament of humiliation, poverty, and political impotence, and the possible remedies, are Professor Mazrui's main concerns. The prime responsibility for this predicament rests with guess whom? The white man, the West. The remedy lies in guess what? The decline of the West and the overthrow of white rule in Southern Africa.

These lectures are thus only another attack on the West by a Western-supported Third World intellectual, one of the most effective I have read. In particular, they are designed to make the greatest impact on Western feelings of guilt.

2

Professor Mazrui writes well. He moves easily between vivid, pertinent episodes and wide political issues. He presents thought-provoking information on various matters as, for instance, the kaleidoscope of African religious belief and the political role of Westernized intellectuals and soldiers. Again, in referring to the brain drain from the Third World, Professor Mazrui rightly notes that this is the result partly of political persecution but mainly of the wish of people to improve their economic position and to explore new vistas. He aptly compares the migration of African intellectuals to the West with that of African traders and workers between African countries for economic betterment. The merits of the book are, however, peripheral. They do not affect the fundamental flaws of the argument.

Professor Mazrui is a skilled political writer. His enterprise involves him in much delicate tightrope walking. He tries to present Africa, as also the Third World, as some sort of actual or potential unity. On his own admission, in Africa there are some 850 distinct ethnic and linguistic groups (p. 92). When talking about Africa he sometimes means the African continent including the Arab north, and at other times he means sub-Saharan Africa; he changes without warning his readers. There is, of course, not even the semblance of unity and uniformity between North Africa and Black Africa. Apart from very limited trade, in historical times their contact was that of intermittent conquest by North Africa of parts of Black Africa and also the much more lasting contact of slave raiding and trading.

The notion of a broadly uniform or united Third World embracing some two-thirds of mankind is fiction. Its acceptance enables Professor Mazrui to bypass such matters as the brutal persecution on ethnic and cultural grounds of large numbers of people in South-East Asia, the Middle East, and, of course, Black Africa itself. In Asia and Africa such large-scale persecution is widespread and evident, including often officially organized and supported racial discrimination. But champions of the Third World, or rather denigrators of the West, such as Professor Mazrui, cannot acknowledge these realities. A united or uniform Africa and a united or uniform Third World are concepts contrived to help to undermine the West and to extract money from it. To present them as anything else involves tergiversation and suppressions.

Professor Mazrui seems anxious to secure the support of the Jewish intelligentsia. He may hope to rebuild the alliance in the United States between the left-liberal Jewish intelligentsia and the black leaders which has disintegrated through the rise of black antisemitism. This latter objective is suggested by his rather forced comparison between Jews and Black Africans and also by his account of the fate of the Jews in Germany, an account which is misleading and also internally inconsistent, but is phrased for maximum political impact (p. 26).

3

Professor Mazrui's paradoxes are no more than different facets of the generally low level of economic performance in Africa. Professor Mazrui attempts to obscure this central fact and to turn it to political advantage. This endeavour is assisted by ignorance, guilt, and confusion in the West. Most people do not appreciate the low level of economic achievement of the indigenous human resources of Africa. If they know it, they tend to feel responsible, or are made to feel responsible, for it.

In historical times the achievement of Black Africa (i.e., most of the continent of Africa) has been negligible compared with that of Asia and Europe. This in no way justifies enslavement or humiliation. But its recognition is indispensable for an understanding of the African scene and for an assessment of Professor Mazrui's discussion.

The fact that a million or so years ago an important stage in evolution may have taken place in Africa has nothing to do with what has happened there in historical times. If the Garden of Eden has decayed, it is because its inhabitants have neglected it. Before the closing decades of the nineteenth century Professor Mazrui's erstwhile Garden of Eden was without the rudiments either of civilized or of modern life. For instance, before the arrival of Europeans in sub-Saharan Africa all transport was by muscle, almost entirely human muscle, unaided by the wheel. There was no public security, man-made roads or ports, Western-type science or technology. All this and much else came with the Europeans in the nineteenth century or even later. Except for the most cursory mention, unrelated to the central argument, Professor Mazrui does not discuss conditions in precolonial Africa or in Liberia, which never was a colony, or social-economic conditions in Ethiopia, independent for thousands of years except for six years as an Italian colony.

Professor Mazrui does not inquire about the personal, social, and political determinants of economic achievement and progress. Achievement is somehow visited on some people but not on others. He writes that as a result of the Industrial Revolution "economic pre-eminence was bestowed upon the countries of Europe and North America" (p. 5). He does not consider the personal attributes and motivations, the social and political conditions, and the many centuries of Western progress before the eighteenth century which were behind the Industrial Revolution. Disregard of background and antecedent history, characteristic of much contemporary social and political discussion, underlies Professor Mazrui's argument and vitiates it.

Why have the Africans not developed their mineral resources? Why did they have to wait for Europeans to explore, develop, process, and market them? Contrary to what Professor Mazrui writes, material backwardness amidst ample natural resources is not anomalous, paradoxical, or surprising. It is familiar both from history and from the contemporary world—witness the American Indians before Columbus, and the contemporary aborigines and pygmies, all extremely backward amidst ample physical resources. Conversely, rapid advance and large-scale achievement of societies with negligible physical resources should also be familiar, as for instance Venice, the Low Countries, Germany, Britain, Japan, and, more recently, Hong Kong, Singapore, and Taiwan. The physical resources of advanced countries were developed by their peoples, as for instance the reclaiming of large parts of Holland and Flanders from the sea and, more generally, improving the land. African backwardness amidst ample natural resources is only one conspicuous example of the fact that material progress depends on personal qualities, social institutions and mores, and political arrangements which make for endeavour and achievement, not simply physical resources.

The relative lack of able and effective people is crucial. This has long been so, although the unpropitious past is no sure basis for predicting the future. What Shiva Naipaul says about Zambia in his recent informative book *North of South: An African Journey* applies widely in Black Africa:

Expatriates staff the mines, the medical services, the factories, the technical colleges, the universities. Without them, the country would fall apart. Zambia makes nothing: Zambia creates nothing. The expatriate lecturer in English waved apologetically at the handful of books, perhaps half a dozen on the library shelf. 'There,' he said. 'that's it. That's all the Zambian literature there is.' For him, the paucity is a source of genuine embarrassment. 'I would dearly love to teach something Zambian to my students. But what can I do if there's nothing.'[2]

Considerations such as these dispose of Professor Mazrui's paradoxes and most of his argument. But there is much else in his widely applauded lectures which deserves comment.

4

The humiliation and suffering of Africa through colonialism, slavery, and racial discrimination provide a major theme. Slavery did indeed inflict much suffering; colonial conquest was often attended by bloodshed; and many Africans have experienced galling racial discrimination. But Professor Mazrui's discussion is nevertheless unbalanced and misleading. Like many Third World writers, he endows the West with complete monopoly both of historical injustice and of contemporary misconduct.

Professor Mazrui writes at length about the Atlantic slave trade. He does not say that slavery was endemic in Africa and widespread elsewhere before then (witness the etymological connection between slav and slave), nor that the supply of slaves for that trade was organized by Africans and Arabs, as the Europeans bought slaves principally at the ports. Nor does he tell his readers that slavery among Africans continued long after it was abolished in the West. Most significant and revealing is, however, the absence of any reference to the Arab slave trade, which was dreaded far and wide in Africa. The Arab slave trade long preceded the Atlantic slave trade, far outlasted it, and was suppressed only through Western effort. It was also even more cruel because many young male slaves were castrated, one reason why in the Middle East there are not many more descendants of Negro slaves. In his masterly and justly celebrated Introduction to *West African Explorers* (Oxford University Press, 1951) Professor Plumb quotes Karl

---

[2] "The man who writes a book in Zambia—usually a simple tale of tribal life—is immediately whisked away into the higher reaches of the administration. One of the writers represented on the shelf had become a member of the Central Committee of the Party; another had been put in charge of a large state-owned organization. But with the fruits of high office dangling so alluringly before them, Zambia is by no means short of would-be writers." Shiva Naipaul, *North of South: An African Journey* (London, André Deutsch, 1978), pp. 233–34.

Barth's observation on this: "Allah had been kind if ten out of one hundred boys survived the operation." Yet Arabs do not feel guilty, nor are they made to feel guilty, about their role in the slave trade. To say anything about the Arab slave trade might be thought to reflect on the solidarity of the Third World; and thus to impair its ability to confront and mulct the West. A feeling of guilt is genuinely a monopoly of the West.

Professor Mazrui must be well-informed about the Arab slave trade and accordingly well qualified to write about it. He comes from Mombasa, a former Arab slave port. The Mazrui of Mombasa were some of the principal slave traders out of that port when Mombasa was part of the dominions of the Sultanate of Oman in the eighteenth and nineteenth centuries.[3]

He also suggests that Western capitalists ceased to support slavery only because hired labour became cheaper and more efficient. Why then did the abolitionists insist on suppressing slavery when it was uneconomic and therefore indeed doomed to disappear?

Extermination is another Western monopoly. Professor Mazrui cites the treatment of the Jews by the Nazis, and that of the American Indians and the Australian aborigines by the Whites. He does not mention in this context the large-scale massacres in Africa, including the early wars of the Zulus, or the slaughter of the Ibo by the Hausa as recently as 1966. These instances are rather more pertinent to Africa.[4]

We have seen that Professor Mazrui regards the outcome of colonialism as a nightmare. Yet it was under colonial rule that the rudiments of modern economic and social life, including public security, disease control, and the suppression of slave raiding were introduced into Black Africa, and which enabled millions of Africans to live longer.

Like so many others, Professor Mazrui interprets colonial experience entirely from the standpoint of the Westernized intellectuals. Many Westernized Africans (whose Westernization by definition came about through the European impact) may have felt humiliated. But may they not have been irked largely because, under colonial rule, they did not enjoy the status, power, and jobs which they claimed because they were educated or at any rate articulate? Under colonial rule, especially British colonial rule, there were relatively few jobs for them, partly because the government was alien, but also because government was so light and limited. What most ordinary people must have felt during the colonial period was that their lives and property were much safer than formerly, and that they were much less affected by disease. To most people such matters are of primary, even para-

---

[3] See a communication on this subject by Dr. J. B. Kelly, *Encounter* (August 1980).

[4] Professor Mazrui does mention the genocidal wars between the Hutu and the Tutsi in Rwanda and Burundi. But even for these he blames the Europeans for not having incorporated these countries into Tanganyika after World War I (*The African Condition,* p. 107).

mount, concern. Obafemi Awolowo, a prominent Nigerian politician of the early postwar years, recognized this in his book *Path to Nigerian Freedom:*

> Given a choice from among white officials, Chiefs and educated Nigerians, as the principal rulers of the country, the illiterate man, today, would exercise his preference for the three in the order in which they are named. He is convinced, *and he has good reason to be,* that he can always get better treatment from the white man than he could hope to get from the Chiefs and the educated elements.[5]

Among the alleged economic ill-effects of colonial rule Professor Mazrui mentions (in a chapter titled "The Burden of Underdevelopment") the production of cash export crops:

> Important biases in the direction of development included, first, the export bias. . . . Cash crops for export were given priority against food for local people. One quarter to one third of the total cultivated areas in some of the more fertile colonies were devoted to the production of such export commodities as cocoa in Ghana, coffee in Uganda, groundnuts in Senegal and the Gambia. . . . (p. 18)

These cash crops have always been cultivated on their own properties by Africans. Cash crops sometimes replace food crops, but in Africa they are often added to food crops, as over much of Africa agricultural production is limited not by land but by labour, and farmers can and often do add cash crops to food (subsistence) crops by working more. But whether they replaced food crops or were grown in addition to food crops, the cultivation of cash crops greatly raised African incomes. Indeed, it was a prime instrument of material advance and helped to transform existence over large areas. Before 1886 there was not one cocoa tree in British West Africa. By the 1930s there were millions of acres under cocoa there, all owned and operated by Africans. Nor were the cash crops grown on fertile or often previously cultivated land; large tracts of jungle or semidesert were turned into productive land. Professor Mazrui does not acknowledge the key role of cash crops in the progress of much of Black Africa, especially West Africa. Africans produce these crops for the same reason that Professor Mazrui, I, and our colleagues teach at universities instead of growing corn or planting potatoes. To condemn cash crops is to patronize the producers by saying that they do not know what is good for them, or that they ought not to have higher incomes.

Incidentally, Professor Mazrui fails to mention that in several African states government policies have affected food production so adversely that

---

[5] Quoted in Frederick Pedler, *Main Currents of West African History 1940–78* (London: Macmillan, 1979), p. 265 (italics added).

the countries have become largely dependent on imported food; and it is not because domestic resources have been diverted to more productive uses. Examples include Mozambique, Tanzania, and Zaire.

In colonialism also Europeans enjoy a monopoly of evil or misconduct. Professor Mazrui does not even mention the extremely brutal Moslem conquest of the Sudan in the early nineteenth century, long before the Congress of Berlin. This conquest was attended by massive and ruthless maltreatment of the blacks in the Southern Sudan unparalleled in nineteenth-century European colonialism, and much of it continued into the 1970s. Nor does Professor Mazrui mention the oppression of the tribal groups, the great majority of the population, by the coastal black rulers of Liberia, nor that of the lording of Amharics over the Galle in Ethiopia, nor the many similar examples of internal tyranny by one African group or another. And further, he fails to note the large numbers of Black Africans who, as we shall see, have been forced to leave their countries.

In the discussion of racism the whites continue as the sole evil-doers. But the villains of racism are of course the whites of Southern Africa. It is not intended as a defence of apartheid to say that his treatment is altogether distorted. Professor Mazrui speaks of "the martyrdom of Sharpeville and the heroism of Soweto" (p. 39). It is disputable whether the people killed there were martyrs to a cause, or part of an uncontrollable mob looting and burning mostly African properties, rather like the mobs in the riots in Accra (Gold Coast, January 1948) and Enugu (Nigeria, November 1949) in which many people were also killed. But what is not in doubt is that those killed in Sharpeville and Soweto together were a small fraction of the numbers of Ibo massacred in Northern Nigeria in 1966 well before the Biafran war; and a much smaller fraction still of the number of Africans killed in the 1960s and 1970s in the struggles between rulers and ruled, some involving genocide, in Rwanda and Burundi, in the Southern Sudan and the Nigerian Civil War. The casualties in Sharpeville and Soweto together were in the hundreds; those killed in these other struggles numbered in the tens of thousands.

Professor Mazrui speaks of the "vast numbers that have been running away either from racial discrimination or racial warfare in Zimbabwe, Namibia or South Africa" (p. 13). However, he seems oblivious—at least to judge from his book—of the large numbers of Black Africans who have been forced to leave their newly independent African countries. Thus in the three Guineas (Guinea, Guinea-Bissau, and Equatorial Guinea) high proportions of the population have been obliged to take refuge abroad. According to an article by Antony Delius (*Times Literary Supplement,* 18 February 1977) about one-quarter of the population of Sekou Toure's Guinea have fled the country and live as refugees in other African states. According to an article in *The Times* of 3 November 1978, approximately one-third of the population of Equatorial Guinea "is in exile, usually in very difficult conditions." And many people fled from Guinea-Bissau after the postindependence massacres.

On the other hand, until the outbreak of guerilla warfare, the African refugees from the white-ruled areas of Southern Africa were confined to a small number of political activists. The numbers involved were a tiny fraction of those who were affected in the Guineas, and also of those who entered white-ruled Southern Africa from elsewhere in Black Africa, at times from as far away as Nigeria. Many more wished, and still wish, to come. They are stopped by immigration restrictions introduced to prevent South Africa and Rhodesia (Zimbabwe) from being flooded by would-be entrants. They are obstructed also by various restrictions in Black Africa designed to stop people from leaving for Southern Africa, as this is politically embarrassing to the rulers.[6] Africans migrate to Southern Africa, or try to get there, because they earn more; their lives and property are much safer; and often because the health and educational facilities are greatly superior.

Professor Mazrui refers to the position of the blacks of South Africa as akin to slavery. It must be unique in history that large numbers of people from all over a huge area wish to travel long distances in the face of formidable obstacles to become slaves.

Even among intellectuals the movement has not been one way. Professor Mazrui mentions Ezekiel Mphahlele, a former South African political activist. "He lived and worked in Zambia, Nigeria and Kenya. He left Africa somewhat disenchanted" and "decided it was time to go home—and suffer with the people. He had decided to come to terms with Africa's paradox of habitation" (p. 13). May he not have returned because he found that with all the humiliation of apartheid South Africa was a better place for him than Zambia, Nigeria, and Kenya, where he had worked? Miss Noni Jabavu is a black South African woman. She wrote *Drawn in Colour* (London, John Murray, 1960), a sensitive and informative description of life in East Africa and Southern Africa, with a faithful account of the humiliations of apartheid, especially petty apartheid. She lived in East Africa. She was married to a prominent English liberal. She was a friend of Andrew Cohen's and his guest when he was governor of Uganda. She returned to live in South Africa because life for a black intellectual there was so much more varied, rich, and safe than in East Africa.

---

[6] Such restrictions which I have not seen mentioned in the Western press have been enforced in some black African states since the 1960s. On this subject again Shiva Naipaul is informative: "Many of the youthful unemployed and under-employed of Lusaka gaze with longing towards Rhodesia and South Africa. Several of those I spoke to said they would, if they could, go to these countries to seek work. Naturally, the Zambian government cannot allow that to happen" (ibid., p. 232).

Professor Mazrui is also out of focus in thinking that white rule in Southern Africa is the overriding problem for Africa as a whole. Much less than one-tenth of the population of Black Africa lives there; many other Blacks would like to go there; and the great majority of the rest are quite unconcerned with Southern Africa, about which most of them know nothing, often not even that it exists.

Indeed, even in the African states adjacent to Southern Africa people at large are quite unconcerned about white supremacy and liberation in South Africa. To quote Shiva Naipaul again:

Rhodesia and South Africa arouse more passion in the West than they do among the citizenry of the black "front-line" states. The shelves of one Lusaka supermarket I went into were laden with South African merchandise—meat, toilet paper, detergents, tinned goods of all kinds. . . . As I strolled along the alleyways of the Lusaka supermarket, I reflected ruefully on the crises of conscience occasioned in the past by my consumption of South African oranges. (p. 231)

Professor Mazrui believes that the world over, ethnic, tribal, and even family ties are on their way out. He regards preferential treatment even of one's close relatives as inappropriate or even improper (p. 44). He ought perhaps to ask the millions of Chinese in Southeast Asia and the Indian refugees from Burma, Sri Lanka, and East Africa, his home base, whether ethnic discrimination in the Third World is disappearing. He might also put his question to many Indians in India. He ignores the massive and brutal persecutions perpetrated by Third World governments on ethnic grounds, often with popular approval. But he seizes upon even trivial instances of ethnic discrimination by whites.

5

What Professor Mazrui writes about the cultural and political scene of Black Africa is sometimes lively and informative. He describes the synchretistic attitudes and practices which incorporate Christian, Islam, and more traditional elements, as for instance in the coexistence of polygamy and monogamy. He also rightly notes important inconsistencies in Western attitudes towards missionary activity. Western missionaries have promoted beliefs and conduct inconsistent with local tradition. But when people from the Third World propagate beliefs and conduct alien to Western mores, they are apt to be ridiculed, persecuted, and even subjected to criminal charges.

Professor Mazrui regards missionary activity as an example of Western penetration of Africa, and more generally of the Third World, which he deplores. He also repeatedly puts forward the interesting suggestion that the

Third World should dispatch its own countermissionaries to the West who might engage in diverse activities, including participation in civil wars, for instance in Ireland and Quebec (p. 16). He looks forward to the decline in the economic and political position of the West. He thinks that the ultimate battles against racial injustice and oppression will be fought "in the streets of Birmingham, ghettos of Detroit, harbours of Marseilles and the motels of the rest of the Western world" (p. 44). These ideas lend particular interest to his proposal. He does not say who is to finance the proposed countermissionaries from the Third World to the West. Many of them would need to be financed from the West, either directly or through the international agencies. They may well come to be so financed—some of them are already, and perhaps Professor Mazrui would include himself among their number.

Professor Mazrui describes vividly the role of the Westernized groups in political life. His examples of the swings in political power between the intellectuals and the military are informative and telling. But he ignores the two principal and indeed decisive factors behind the political prominence of Westernized Africans. One is the absence of a strongly entrenched local culture, such as Hinduism or Islam, more resistant to Western impact. The second factor was the increasing readiness of the Western powers in the 1940s and 1950s to accept the articulate Westernized groups as the representatives of Africa. This was crucial in the political sphere. In British policy this was a complete reversal of the previous practice of trying to build on traditional and specifically local forms of authority in preparation for independence.

The most influential ideologies in the West since the 1930s consistently favoured the articulate Westernized and urbanized groups in Africa. They also favoured extensive economic controls. As a result, closely controlled economies were handed over to the incoming African governments in which these Westernized groups predominated. Since World War II these preferences have continued to shape the policies of the official international organizations and aid agencies. Unwilling and powerless populations have thereby come to be placed at the mercy of their unrepresentative rulers.

Professor Mazrui correctly notes that Western-style government was inappropriate to African conditions, even though its debut there was widely applauded in the 1950s and 1960s. But he does not seem to remember that Westernized Africans had pressed for these Western-type parliamentary systems. They claimed that other arrangements would have given power to so-called reactionary elements, that is, traditional authorities such as local chiefs and councils. They claimed also that to deny Western-style political arrangements to the incoming independent governments would be evidence of Western feelings of superiority.

The extensive economic controls promoted in the closing years of colonial rule, and subsequently also by various Western aid programmes, vastly increased the gains and losses in the fight for political power. This result in turn provoked conflict and has encouraged centrifugal forces, the suppression of which required much coercion, often accompanied by large-scale civil war and bloodshed. Western policy since World War II therefore not only hastened the collapse of Westminster-style government in Africa, but also ensured that it would be succeeded by kleptocracy, conflict, and despotism.

Professor Mazrui regrets to some extent the prominence of the Westernized groups in Africa in which he sees yet another example of Western influence. But he nevertheless interprets African experience virtually wholly in terms of their concerns and interests. This is why he says that the European impact on Africa was a nightmare, or that the production of cash crops by Africans harmed them, when in fact these sequences transformed for the better the lives of many millions of Africans.

Like many other Westernized Africans, notably including Kwame Nkrumah, Professor Mazrui attributes the economical and political weakness of Africa largely to its fragmentation into fifty or more different states; and again like others, including Nkrumah, he blames the West for this. This figure includes the North African countries, which have nothing in common with Black Africa, except for occasional concerted action against the West, especially under UN and UNCTAD auspices. The multiplicity of Black African states is the result of ethnic and tribal diversity, which in turn reflects the age-old isolation of small and warring communities, brought about by the absence even of rudimentary transport facilities and public security. By providing transport facilities and public security Western activities have in fact broken down this isolation over large areas and have thus helped to create larger communities.

The state-controlled economies of recent decades have to some extent worked in the opposite direction. By greatly increasing the prizes of political power, state economic controls encourage separatist tendencies in heterogeneous societies. Simultaneously, they make the rulers more reluctant to cooperate with one another, as such cooperation implies some surrender of their power over their subjects. But the articulate Westernized Africans have consistently pressed for Western help to establish and operate extensive state controls.

6

Professor Mazrui often refers to East Africa where he comes from and where he taught for many years. Dr. Nyerere is accorded the usual uncritical adulation. He is, of course, referred to as a front-line president (p. 108), although Tanzania has no common frontier with Zimbabwe-Rhodesia. He is described as "humane, sophisticated and sensitive to the wider implications of every act of policy" (p. 111), and again, "Julius Nyerere does not believe in summary justice in his domestic policies. He is in reality a liberal democrat with a socialist veneer" (p. 110). During Nyerere's regime there have been numerous political killings in Tanzania. People have been incarcerated without trial for long periods in harsh conditions. Millions of people have been forced into collectivized villages, often mere sites, far from their homes. Those who tried to resist have had their homesteads razed and were themselves deprived of elementary comforts and civil rights.[7] Expropriations are frequent. But all this is forgiven, perhaps because President Nyerere is hostile to the West, to personal freedom and property, and to individual farming and private enterprise.

Professor Mazrui also explicitly commends Nyerere's foreign policy, which he regards as the attempted establishment of Pax Tanzaniana, in turn a stepping stone to a Pax Africana. Components of the Pax Tanzaniana, noted on the whole approvingly by Professor Mazrui, have included the support of the bloody coup in Zanzibar with its butchery of hundreds of people; assistance to the left-wing coup in the Seychelles; forcible closure of the border with Kenya, which inflicted much hardship on the local people, but which was apparently intended "to teach the government of Nairobi a lesson through economic means" (p. 108). What lesson? Perhaps to force the Kenyatta government to adopt internal policies similar to those of President Nyerere.

Establishment of the Pax Tanzaniana involved also the invasion of Amin's Uganda. Professor Mazrui thinks that the original purpose of this exercise was probably modest, no more than to teach Amin a lesson, but that Nyerere was drawn all the way by the lack of effective resistance. Professor Mazrui says nothing about the killing of civilians and the large-scale looting by the Tanzanian troops, long after the overthrow of Amin in April 1979. The Tanzanian army is in February 1980 in Uganda. In Tanzania after many years of massive Western aid living standards are lower than they had been even in Amin's Uganda. The troops may not want to return. Perhaps President Nyerere may not be anxious to have them back after their experiences and activities in Uganda. When in 1964 the Tanzanian army mutinied, Nyerere had to appeal to Britain to suppress the revolt with a handful of troops—another piece of history ignored by the Reith lecturer.

Professor Mazrui repeatedly mentions Amin's oppressive dictatorship. But he does not record that the establishment of a totalitarian regime in Uganda antedated it. In 1966, shortly before the date of an election which

---

[7] A report in the *Washington Post*, 6 May 1975, put the numbers who had to leave their traditional villages at between six and eight million. According to the report this was the largest migration in African history.

he would have lost, Dr. Obote staged an extremely bloody coup followed by civil war, in which, with Western support, he overthrew the popular Kabaka. He promptly suppressed all political parties other than his own and set up a tyrannical regime, which in turn was overthrown by Amin in a bloodless coup in 1971. According to the blurb of the book Professor Mazrui was an important influence on the national politics of Uganda under President Obote.

In reflecting on the prospects of non-Africans after the confidently expected overthrow of white rule in South Africa, Professor Mazrui writes that in the long run there may well be much scope for them, although this is not certain. In this context he writes:

> At least in the urban areas Kenya has successfully maintained a multiracial society. On the other hand, in Uganda Idi Amin ruthlessly threw out thousands of Asians. (p. 18)

Many thousands of Asians and Europeans, including groups who had been there for generations, have had to leave Kenya because, not being indigenous Africans, they were denied economic opportunities. Through the length and breadth of Black Africa postcolonial governments have forced out Asians, Europeans, Levantines, and also Black African "strangers," by refusing to renew employment permits or trading licences.

7

Certain of Professor Mazrui's other themes, which often mirror contemporary ideology and intellectual fashion, bear both on his hopes and proposals and also on their appeal.

In Professor Mazrui's scheme of things, economic achievement and change do not result from people's activities. They simply happen, as did for instance the Industrial Revolution. At times this leads to bizarre statements such as that Zaire "was among the very first African countries to discover uranium" (p. 135). What happened was that Westerners explored and discovered uranium there. Total neglect of human achievement, and of the personal qualities and the social and political circumstances behind it, runs through the lectures, from the unexplained decay of the Garden of Eden in the first lecture to Professor Mazrui's vision of the end of the twentieth century in the last.

Professor Mazrui's lecture on the Burden of Underdevelopment should more correctly be entitled Lack of Economic Achievement. But the role of the determinants of economic performance is exactly what he refuses to acknowledge. This is why he harps on the poverty of Africa amidst ample natural resources.

The continent itself seems to be well endowed with resources, but a disproportionate number of people in the continent is undernourished and underprivileged. A situation where a continent is well endowed but the people are
poor is a situation of anomalous underdevelopment. (p. 72)

There is no anomaly. As I have already insisted, economic achievement
depends on people and their arrangements, not on natural resources.

Professor Mazrui would like Africa to modernize, but without Westernization (pp. 80–82). This is not possible. The concept of material progress,
of steadily increasing control of man over his environment, is Western, as
are the modes of conduct which derive from it. Progress and its conditions
and manifestations may not be laudable or conducive to happiness. But the
idea of modernization without Westernization is self-contradictory.

Professor Mazrui regards income differences as a reflection of unjust privileges and exploitation. Poor individuals, groups, and societies are underprivileged and deprived. Like others who write in this vein he fails to ask
how external forces, especially Western contacts, could possibly have caused
the poverty of the poorest, most backward groups in Africa (pygmies, aborigines, desert people) when these have few outside contacts and no commercial contacts with the West. Throughout Africa, as elsewhere in the
Third World, the level of economic achievement declines with the distance
from the impact of Western commercial contact.

Professor Mazrui's view that poverty means injustice and oppression
clearly implies that poverty reflects misconduct by others. Thus, if blacks are
relatively poor, this is evidence or misconduct by other groups. This corollary lends special interest to his ideas, mentioned earlier, that the struggle
for black liberation must extend beyond South Africa to the West and that
his proposed countermissionaries should participate in civil wars there. On
the other hand, the most backward groups in Africa as well as elsewhere in
the Third World seem to be doubly afflicted. They are extremely poor. They
are also isolated. Thus there is no one from whom they could be liberated.

Professor Mazrui believes that the size of a country, especially when al-
lied to natural resources, confers political power. He envisages that, because
of their size and natural resources, by the end of the twentieth century,
Nigeria, a liberated South Africa, and Zaire will be the diplomatic leaders of
Africa and will also be prominent in world affairs. Size and natural resources
are all. But in fact these confer neither riches nor political power without
appropriate human resources and the will to use them for these purposes.
Neither size nor natural resources conferred power on China or India. Conversely, Venice, Holland, and Britain were world powers when they were
still small and had few natural resources.

According to Professor Mazrui worldwide exhaustion of natural resources
and the population explosion are among the crises which endanger Africa,

the Third World, and indeed the whole world. The West is again the root of all evil. "The Western world already consumes far too much of what there is on the planet, without planning for much more" (p. 115). In accordance with pretentious and fashionable jargon, he is apt to refer to the world as the planet, or the planet earth. Here again, he writes as if goods and services somehow just existed when they are, of course, produced by people. He does not say that Western production not only pays for all Western consumption, but in addition provides capital for the Third World. There is no danger from the exhaustion of physical resources. If a resource becomes relatively scarce, this leads to greater economy in its use and to the development of substitutes. Moreover, with the exception of fossil fuel, all other mineral resources can be largely recovered as scrap. Should all natural resources threaten to give out, which is extremely improbable, human reproductive behaviour will be modified long before their exhaustion.

It is true that the West is behind the population explosion in the Third World. Before the impact of the West, high fertility in the Third World was balanced by correspondingly high mortality. Western science, technology and medicine, and Western-induced economic improvement brought about the steep fall in mortality and the corresponding rise in life expectation there. The population explosion reflects, therefore, a large improvement in conditions because people like to live longer and see their children do so. However, Professor Mazrui somehow manages to connect the population explosion with high child mortality. He presents a harrowing account of half-a-dozen children of one of his friends dying, which forces his friend to have a larger number of children to replace those lost through early death (p. 114). Here again the West is to blame because, according to Professor Mazrui, the high child mortality reflects Western-imposed economic injustice. But, of course, mortality, including child mortality, was far higher before the impact of the West. In recent decades it has declined sharply, and this has brought about the so-called population explosion, a change which, as just noted, is an evident and significant improvement.

Professor Mazrui's treatment of Portuguese colonial rule and of its aftermath is again carefully structured for maximum appeal. He argues that it is because British rule was less repressive and terminated sooner that its successor states are less radically Marxist than are Angola and Mozambique. Special condemnation of Portuguese rule is pleasing not only to general anticolonial sentiment, but perhaps even more to British conservatives, who have always been both baffled and irked by the longer duration of Portuguese rule. The more explicit Marxism of the governments of Angola and Mozambique owes much to such factors as the greater Soviet involvement there and to the Cuban intervention in Angola. In any case, it is questionable whether Nyerere's policies are less collectivist than President Machel's. It is certainly rather eccentric to suggest, as does Professor Mazrui, that President Nyerere is a bourgeois liberal. He also forgets that Nkrumah, the first president of the first successor state to British rule in Africa, was an avowed and practising Marxist-Leninist. Nor does Professor Mazrui say that the present rulers of Ethiopia, who took over an independent state, are of extreme left-wing persuasion and pursue communist policies as far as they can. It is also worth remembering that Nehru had to invade Goa, after refusing its population a plebiscite. Portuguese rule in Africa and Asia has always presented a special problem to antiracists. The Portuguese explicitly encouraged miscegenation and hoped to create mini-Brazils, especially in Angola and Mozambique, a stance which made it difficult to accuse them of racism.

8

Professor Mazrui is an exponent of the economics and politics of resentment. His policy proposals are designed to erode the West and to undermine the whites in Southern Africa, especially in South Africa, rather than to promote the welfare of ordinary Africans. The pursuit of this overriding objective and the disregard of human faculties and mores lead to numerous and evident inconsistencies.

For the time being Professor Mazrui would welcome "some continuing extravagance in the Western world, but this is only a transitional strategy designed to weaken it sufficiently to make it responsive to the demands of global reform" (p. 115). He hopes for more cartels of the OPEC type to exploit Western dependence on external sources of raw material. However, as is widely and rightly recognized, the effectiveness of OPEC owes much to special conditions which are certainly not present in the case of African primary products. Commodity cartels for other such products could not possibly be effective without Western support, including that of Western-financed official international organizations. But perhaps Professor Mazrui, viewing issues and prospects from an exalted position, is not to be bothered with such practicalities or with the major domestic problems of commodity schemes.

Professor Mazrui takes continued foreign aid for granted. He only wishes individual countries to diversify their sources of aid to make them more independent of particular donors. But how is persistent external help consistent with independence and self-reliance? Professor Mazrui does not suggest that the African countries should help themselves, but only that they should help themselves to Western largesse, a practice which does not make for sustained prosperity.

Professor Mazrui proposes extensive replacement of Western imports and foreign personnel, technology, and capital by local resources. Where are these to come from, and who is to pay? Ordinary people in the Third World would either have to pay more for locally produced supplies or go without the goods and services they desire. But Professor Mazrui is not concerned with the economic costs borne by ordinary people or their needs, wants, and preferences. He wishes to replace Western publications and films by local products because he regards their ubiquity as a form of imperialism. In fact, in Africa as elsewhere in the Third World, the proliferation of Western products reflects the preferences of ordinary people, a preference obnoxious to local intellectuals.

Professor Mazrui advocates what he calls horizontal interpenetration of the Third World. In plain English, this means official restriction of commercial contact with the West. Such restrictions deprive people of what they want and can afford. Mutual trade among the very poor and the bankrupt does not promote prosperity. The restrictions also place people even more at the mercy of the rulers than they already are.

African or Third World unity is pure fiction. Neither the spirit nor the resources for concerted action are available without external help. Systematic replacement of Western commercial and cultural contacts by mutual trade and cultural collaboration presupposes external organization and resources. The same applies to concerted political or military action.

Professor Mazrui complains that African communications, including telephones, are oriented to the outside world. The reason is of course that they have been constructed by Westerners and are used by them or by Westernized groups. No external force stopped Africans from developing such facilities. That it is easier to telephone from Kenya to the United States than to West Africa shows again that African unity without outside help is fictitious, that concerted action by African states depends on external resources. All this is stubbornly ignored by Professor Mazrui who refuses to recognize the connection between people and achievement.

Professor Mazrui expects much from the development of the mineral resources of Africa. Indeed, as we have seen, he expects that this will confer international importance and power on some African states, including Zaire and liberated South Africa. But mineral development again presupposes external personnel, technology, and capital, whether from the West or from communist countries.

Professor Mazrui's overriding preoccupation is with the undermining of the West and with the enhancement of the real or illusory political power of the African rulers and perhaps that of their Western advisers acting as court theologians. The power of these rulers will depend on the readiness of the West to provide resources for the erosion of its own position and for the tightening of the grip of these rulers over their own subjects.

The direction of his argument is evident also in his proposals for a complete Western boycott of South Africa and for Western subsidies to guerilla movements. He admits that many people think that contacts with South Africa, especially inflow of capital, erode apartheid. An inflow of capital also promptly improves the lot of Africans by increasing the demand for labour and reducing the relative scarcity of capital, which is primarily a white asset.

Professor Mazrui does not specify whether his proposed boycott of South Africa is to extend to relations between that country and the black African states. Zambia depends heavily on South Africa for food and other consumer goods. Many thousands of people from Mozambique work in South Africa under a little-publicized agreement between the two governments. The South African Railways and Harbour Board is extensively involved in the administration of the Mozambique railway and the port of Maputo.[8] Professor Mazrui does not acquaint his readers with these realities. Shortly before Professor Mazrui began his lectures, the extensive dependence on South Africa of Zambia, Malawi, and Mozambique for technical personnel, food, consumer goods, organization of transport, basic machinery, employment opportunities for black labour, and export routes and facilities was reviewed in an article in the *Financial Times* (15 August 1979). The population of these countries would suffer much hardship from an effective boycott of South Africa.

It is speculative whether apartheid would be eroded more effectively by the inflow of capital and the extension of commercial contacts or by complete boycott of South Africa, if this were practicable, and by large-scale financing of guerilla movements. Professor Mazrui regards violent revolution as the solution for South Africa. Unlike a more gradual process, forcible overthrow of white rule necessarily involves violent conflict and bloodshed. It is also much more likely to unleash tribal war and large-scale maltreatment of Asians. This last outcome is likely to be conspicuous because in South Africa, as in Central and East Africa, Africans at large dislike the Asians much more than they do the whites. This is another matter habitually swept under the carpet by exponents of Third World solidarity and one about which Shiva Naipaul again writes with candour:

> As is the case all over East and Central Africa, it is not the whites who arouse the greatest animosity, but the Asians. My stay coincided with a vigorous anti-Asian campaign in the Zambian press. Day after day, in the Times of Zambia, lengthy articles and impassioned letters to the Editor were devoted to this enthralling subject. Asian women were accused of harbouring feelings of superiority because they did not sleep with or marry Zambian men. Photographs were published showing suitcases filled to the brim with bank notes seized from Asians attempting to smuggle currency out of the country. Asian businessmen,

[8] The economy of Mozambique would probably collapse if it did not allow South African technicians to operate its ports and railways and encourage substantial numbers of its citizens to work in the mines of the "enemy." Naipaul, *North of South*, p. 232.

predictably enough, were guilty of monopolising the distributive trades and ex-
ploiting innocent Zambians. Could Asians, one letter writer wanted to know,
ever become patriots? The climax came with the front-page headline which
read: 'Asian Doctors Kill their Patients'. . . . Hounding the Asian is a legitimate
blood-sport; a national pastime. On another page of the same newspaper then
was a photograph of Indira Gandhi, who, a day or two previously, had been in
Lusaka preaching the gospel of Afro-Asian solidarity. Afro-Asian solidarity
aside, a man from Mars would have no trouble in deducing that Asians, not
Rhodesians, not South Africans, were the overriding threat to the security and
well-being of the Zambian State and Zambian people. (pp. 232–33)

The fate of the Asians after violent revolution in South Africa would not
be enviable. But such matters are of little moment to Professor Mazrui.
Writings such as Professor Mazrui's Reith Lectures have been helpful to
the determined supporters of apartheid within South Africa. They can
make political capital out of them by arguing that their critics are ignorant
or malicious.

9

The African scene does indeed present a baffling anomaly or paradox. But
this is very different from Professor Mazrui's pseudo parodoxes and is
indeed their opposite.

How does it come about that African rulers whose military and economic resources are negligible are yet taken seriously, and exercise such influence as, say, President Nyerere? Why does the West abase itself before
him or Mr. Kaunda, rulers whose own resources are extremely meagre, and
who could not survive without large-scale Western help? One factor is the
unfounded but widespread and much articulated feeling of guilt in the
West. Conflict and dissension in the West is another. There are many people in the West who have come to dislike, or even to hate, their own society and its institutions, or who long for more money and power or for
greater status. They often look to Third World spokesmen and politicians
as allies or instruments in a civil conflict. Mere ignorance does not explain
prevailing attitudes because ignorance by itself is neutral and does not
therefore account for a particular slant of opinion. Such influences may also
explain the adulation of President Nyerere; the references to Dr. Ramphal
as the man who saved Rhodesia; the commendations of Mr. Kaunda, and
of his meaningless vapourings about so-called African humanism; and the
references to Professor Mazrui as a formidable mind and as an author capable of Byronic presentation. The effectiveness of such praise and flattery is
enhanced because those who proffer them act as a claque. The operation

VIII

Ecclesiastical Economics: Envy Legitimized

> After Pryde wol I speken of the foule sinne of Envye, which
> is, as by the word of the philosophre, sorwe [sorrow] of
> other mannes prosperitee.
>
> *Chaucer, The Parson's Tale*

1

Envy is traditionally one of the seven deadly sins. Vocal modern clerical opinion endows it with moral legitimacy and intellectual respectability. The results of this specious legitimization of envy are the principal themes of this chapter.

2

Since World War II, prominent clergymen and theologians have been much preoccupied with domestic and international differences in income and wealth. A broad consensus has emerged, and its supporters range from recent popes to explicitly Marxist clerics.

The following are the central theme and its supporting arguments. Social justice requires that incomes should be substantially equal; appreciable differences in incomes reflect exploitation, oppression, discrimination, or improper privilege; and politically organized redistribution is desirable, or even a Christian duty. These opinions are particularly common, insistent, and strident in discussions on economic differences between the West and the Third World and on those within individual Third World countries.

I shall discuss these opinions primarily by examining two influential documents by Pope Paul VI: the Encyclical Letter, *Populorum Progressio* (1967), and the Pontifical Letter, *Octogesima Adveniens* (1971), referred to hereafter as the papal documents or letters. The two documents must be treated synoptically as the latter relies heavily on the former, which is also generally more explicit than its successor.[1]

This essay originally appeared in the *American Enterprise Institute*, July 1981.
[1] Throughout essay, *Populorum Progressio* will be cited parenthetically as *PP*, and *Octogesima Adveniens* as *OA*. The numbers in parentheses in the text refer to the numbered paragraphs in these documents. The passages are quoted from the official English texts published

of this claque reinforces the impact of the opinions it supports and simultaneously smothers dissenting voices. There are many thousands of people in the West who have heard of Professor Mazrui for every one who has heard of Miss Noni Jabavu, whose book is far more informative than are Professor Mazrui's lectures.

Such forces presumably explain also how he came to be invited to give the Reith Lectures, the most widely publicized lectures in Britain. In this instance they were also particularly expensive to produce because, as Professor Mazrui acknowledges, he received generous financial support from the BBC for two extensive tours in Africa.

10

His book is published under an educational imprint which I first encountered when reading *Africa Must Unite,* a collection of Nkrumah's outpourings. Professor Mazrui is much more sophisticated than Nkrumah was, but his lectures are of no greater intellectual substance. It is misleading to call such books educational. But then this could also be said of expressions such as the United Nations, the British Commonwealth, the German Democratic Republic, and many others. Professor Mazrui's book only reconfirms that the world language of the late twentieth century is not English: it is Newspeak.

3

The main theme of the papal documents is that economic differences, consistently termed inequalities, reflect injustice.

According to these papal documents, substantial economic differences reflect the perversion of that just and natural state which is to be expected from the fact that God has created the earth for all mankind and created man in his image. The differences result from the exploitation and oppression of the weak by the strong, including denial of opportunities to the former by the latter.

The Pope quotes the Second Vatican Council: "God intended the earth and all that it contains for the use of every human being and people" (*PP,* 22). He then quotes St. Ambrose: "You are not making a gift of your possessions to the poor person. You are handing over to him what is his. For what has been given in common for the use of all, you have arrogated to yourself. The world is given to all, and not only to the rich" (*PP,* 23).

These passages are reproduced on posters and in leaflets in numerous churches in the West. Often they refer particularly to the Third World, usually in terms such as that the earth belongs to all its peoples, yet at the same time three-quarters of them do not share in it.

Subsidiary themes support the main theme, that inequality means injustice. A major problem is the question of "the fairness in the exchange of goods and in the division of wealth between individuals and countries" (*OA,* 7). The economic system left to itself widens international economic differences: "rich peoples enjoy rapid growth whereas the poor develop slowly. The imbalance is on the increase: some produce a surplus of foodstuffs, others cruelly lack them and see their exports made uncertain" (*PP,* 8).

Again, "in trade between developed and underdeveloped economies, conditions are too disparate and the degrees of genuine freedom available

---

by Polyglot Press, Vatican City, in 1967 and 1971. Unless stated otherwise, references to the Pope are to Paul VI. Some of the passages I quote incorporate statements from other prominent Catholic sources. As these statements are accepted and endorsed by the Pope, I shall usually not refer to the original sources but quote them as expressions of the Pope's views. Pope John Paul II seems to share the central opinions on economic matters of his recent predecessors. This is suggested by the encyclical *Laborem Exercens,* 1981, which is, however, less calculated to arouse envy and resentment than the encyclicals of Paul VI. I shall not on this occasion quote Protestant clergymen or theologians. Elsewhere, I have examined some opinions by Professor Ronald J. Sider, a prominent evangelical churchman, on the subject of economic differences between the West and the Third World. His opinions are typical of much contemporary evangelical thought. He is quoted extensively in the chapter entitled "Western Guilt and Third World Poverty." in *Equality, the Third World and Economic Delusion,* edited by P. T. Bauer, London and Cambridge, Mass., 1981.

too unequal" (*PP,* 61). This inequality is responsible for the persistent deterioration in the terms of trade of primary producers. "The value of manufactured goods is rapidly increasing and they can always find an adequate market. On the other hand, raw materials produced by underdeveloped countries are subject to wide and sudden fluctuations in price, a state of affairs far removed from the progressively increasing value of industrial products. . . . The poor nations remain ever poor while the rich ones become still richer" (*PP,* 57).

In some cases the difficulties are legacies of colonialism. The colonial rulers have sometimes "left a precarious economy bound up for instance with the production of one kind of crop whose market prices are subject to sudden and considerable variation" (*PP,* 7).

The situation calls for urgent action: "We must make haste: too many are suffering, and the distance is growing that separates the progress of some and the stagnation, not to say the regression, of others" (*PP,* 29).

Both within countries and also on the international plane, inequalities of wealth go hand in hand with inequalities of power: "There is also the scandal of glaring inequalities not merely in the enjoyment of possessions but even more in the exercise of power. While a small restricted group enjoys a refined civilization in certain regions, the remainder of the population, poor and scattered, is deprived of nearly all possibility of personal initiative and of responsibility, and often times even its living and working conditions are unworthy of the human person" (*PP,* 9).

The Pope refers also to "unproductive monopolization of resources by a small number of men" (*PP,* 66). All these differences lead to "social conflicts which have taken on world dimensions" (*PP,* 9).

Specific groups are singled out for condemnation. They include landowners whose "landed estates impede the general prosperity because they are extensive, unused or poorly used, or because they bring hardship to peoples or are detrimental to the interests of the country (so that the common good sometimes demands their expropriation)." There are also people who transfer part of their money "abroad purely for their own advantage, without care for the manifest wrong they inflict on their country by doing this" (*PP,* 24).

There are those who create superfluous wants, so that while "very large numbers of people are unable to satisfy their primary needs, superfluous needs are ingeniously created"(*OA,* 9). There are those who derive "inadmissible profits" through speculation in necessities (*OA,* 10). Leaders of multinational enterprises are chided for returning to "inhuman principles of individualism when they operate in less developed countries" (*PP,* 70).

There are also specific categories of victims of injustice. These include people who cannot find "a decent dwelling at a price they can afford' (*OA,* 11); and those "who are denied the right to work [at] equitable remuneration" (*OA,* 14).

Suggestions or hints for action are scattered about in the two documents. The suggestions are often extremely vague and at times implicit rather than explicit. However, the general direction is clear. It is along the following lines.

Christians must do their best in a spirit of charity to remedy the injustice of social, cultural, and especially economic differences, which, according to the Pope, at times cries to heaven. Individual action is insufficient to deal with the problems. Collective action is required and to be effective has to be political. This is so partly because of the magnitude of the problems. Another even more important reason why action has to be collective and political is that, in the explicit opinion of the Pope, governments always act for the common good (*OA,* 46, quoted below). The efforts should take the form primarily of concerted international actions and plans.

The proposals revolve around the theme of politically organized redistribution. The primary theme is the urgent need for official international wealth transfers to redress existing international inequality and injustice and thereby to promote development and peace.

These official transfers are necessary "to further the progress of poorer peoples, to encourage social justice among nations, to offer to less developed nations the means whereby they can further their own progress" (*PP,* 5). For this purpose "all available resources should be pooled" (*PP,* 43).

"Advanced nations have a very heavy obligation to help the developing peoples. . . . Every nation must produce more and better quality goods to give to all its inhabitants a truly human standard of living, and also to contribute to the common development of the human race" (*PP,* 48).

"We must repeat once more that the superfluous wealth of rich countries should be placed at the service of poor nations. The rule which up to now held good for the benefit of those nearest to us, must today be applied to all the needy of this world. Besides, the rich will be the first to benefit as a result. Otherwise their continued greed will certainly call down upon them the judgment of God and the wrath of the poor, with consequences no one can foretell" (*PP,* 49).

"May everyone be convinced of this: the very life of poor nations, civil peace in developing countries, and world peace itself are at stake" (*PP,* 55).

In international trade, major changes are required to rectify the inequality of bargaining power between the West and the Third World and the lack of genuine economic freedom of the latter. International agreements "would establish general norms for regulating certain prices, for guaranteeing certain types of production, for supporting certain new industries" (*PP,* 61). "Internationally organized investment, production, trade, and education would help to create employment in countries where population is growing rapidly" (*OA,* 18).

Other suggestions for international action include technical assistance to less developed countries, and regional agreements among weak nations for mutual support (*PP,* 71, 77).

The Pope writes under the heading "Development is the New Name for Peace": "Excessive economic, social and cultural inequalities among peoples arouse tensions and conflicts, and are a danger to peace. . . . To wage war on misery and to struggle against injustice is to promote, along with improved conditions, the human and spiritual progress of all men, and therefore the common good of humanity. Peace cannot be limited to a mere absence of war" (*PP,* 76).

The United Nations has a key role "to bring not some people but all peoples to treat each other as brothers. . . . Who does not see the necessity of thus establishing progressively a world authority capable of acting effectively in the juridical and political sectors?" (*PP,* 78). "Some would consider such hopes Utopian. It may be . . . that they have not perceived the dynamism of the world which desires to live more fraternally" (*PP,* 79).

The Pope also envisages far-reaching policies within countries to promote progress and to remedy injustice: "Development demands bold transformations, innovations that go deep. Urgent reforms should be undertaken without delay" (*PP,* 32). "As we have seen, these reforms will include expropriation of the properties of at least some categories of landowners" (*PP,* 24).

Under the heading "Programmes and Planning" the Pope writes: "It pertains to the public authorities to choose, even to lay down, the objectives to be pursued in economic development, the ends to be achieved, and the means of attaining them, and it is for them to stimulate all the forces engaged in this common activity" (*PP,* 33). These tasks must be left to governments, to the representatives of political power, "which is the natural and necessary link for ensuring the cohesion of the social body. . . . It always intervenes with careful justice and with devotion to the common good for which it holds final responsibility" (*OA,* 46).

The ultimate aim is to build a world where "every man, no matter what his race, religion, or nationality, can live a full human life, freed from servitude imposed upon him by other men or by natural forces over which he has not sufficient control; a world where freedom is not an empty word and where the poor man Lazarus can sit down at the same table with the rich man" (*PP,* 47).

4

The Pope's diagnosis and proposals are remarkably commonplace. There is nothing distinctively Christian or Catholic about them. They were already in vogue when the pronouncements were issued, and they are still in vogue today.[2] They are to be found, for example, in so secular a document as the Brandt report, *North-South: A Programme for Survival.*

Third World Catholic opinions on these matters are particularly notable because by the end of the century the great majority of Catholics are likely to be in the Third World, primarily Latin America. Here are some examples, which again I shall quote without at this point examining their validity.

According to Monsenor Alfonso Lopez Trujillo, the secretary general of the Latin American Bishops' Conference: "The United States and Canada are rich because the peoples of Latin America are poor. They have built their wealth on top of us."[3]

Dom Helder Camara, known as Brother of the Poor or the Red Bishop, has become an international figure with speaking engagements all over the world. In an interview with the London-based magazine *South* (December 1980) headed "The Church that Refuses to Think for the Poor," he is reported as saying:

> But it [rural poverty] is not a local problem: it is a national problem, even a continental problem. You know that the prices of our raw materials have always been set in the great decision-making centres of the world. . . . And while we [the Catholic Church] supported what amounted to social disorder, the United Nations were proclaiming that two-thirds of mankind live in inhuman conditions of misery and hunger.

Dr. Julius Nyerere, president of Tanzania (and a Catholic), said in London a few years ago:

> In one world, as in one state, when I am rich because you are poor, and I am poor because you are rich, the transfer of wealth from the rich to the poor is a matter of right; it is not an appropriate matter for charity. . . . If the rich nations go on getting richer and richer at the expense of the poor, the poor of the world must demand a change in the same way as the proletariat in the rich countries demanded a change in the past.[4]

---

[2] The modishness, one might say trendiness, of the papal documents is evident throughout. Section headings include "Women," "Environment," and "Development—A New Name for Peace." The documents also, unsurprisingly, discuss such topics as debt rescheduling, commodity agreements, and rent controls—in every instance at an amateur, populist level.

[3] Quoted by Malcolm Deas, "Catholics and Marxists," *London Review of Books,* 19 March 1981.

[4] Julius Nyerere, "The Economic Challenge: Dialogue or Confrontation." *African Affairs,* London, April 1976.

Finally, I offer an example from an influential source which explicitly brings in the multinational companies. Peter Nichols, Rome correspondent of *The Times* (London), wrote in his much-publicized book *The Pope's Divisions* (London 1981): "Much of the economy [of Latin America] is dominated by multinationals who take out basic raw materials in return for impossible wages."[5]

5

Income differences cannot be discussed sensibly without looking at their background. Individuals, groups, and societies can be poor for any number of different reasons. Thus a person may become poor because he has habitually overspent a large income; or he may be poor for circumstances entirely beyond his control such as incurable disease, confiscation of his assets, or the restriction of his opportunities. Individuals and groups may be materially unambitious. Contrast for instance the conduct and position of Malays and Chinese in Malaysia. Again, if many poor people survive longer in an LDC, this depresses *per capita* incomes and leads to what is habitually termed a worsening of income distribution, both within the particular country and relative to richer countries. Conversely, if more of the poor die or a society reverts to subsistence production, this brings about more equal incomes within a country, accompanied by a rise in *per capita* incomes in the former case and a decline in the latter case.

In egalitarian discourse, the notion that the well-off have prospered at the expense of the poor is rarely far below the surface, a notion which is useful or even necessary for the moral plausibility of politically organized redistribution. Without such an underpinning, the case for redistributive taxation (which in effect is partial confiscation) or for other forms of expropriation is not self-evident. Why should social justice mean substantially equal incomes? Why is it obviously unjust that those who contribute more to production should have higher incomes than those who contribute less?

The case for politically organized redistribution becomes yet more dubious when it is remembered that this policy is apt to aggravate the lot of the poorest as well as to aggrandize those who organize the transfers. To begin with, state-organized redistribution often benefits middle-income groups at the expense both of the rich and of the poor. This is now widely recognized in the context of redistribution within a country, especially when the benefits accruing to the administrators of these policies are also taken into account. Moreover, redistribution inhibits enterprise and effort

---

[5] Quoted by Deas, "Catholics and Marxists."

and the accumulation and productive deployment of capital, and this result retards a rise in living standards, including those of the poorest.

The adverse effects of redistribution on the living standards of the poorest are perforce ignored when income and wealth are envisaged, as they often are, as being extracted from other people, or somehow achieved at their expense by depriving them of what they had or could have had. They are regarded as fixed totals rather than as the results of productive activities and processes over time. In market economies, however, incomes are normally earned; they are not shares in a preexisting total.

Group differences in economic performance abound in the Third World. In Malaysia, for instance, Chinese economic performance has for many years been far superior to that of Malays in spite of long-standing discrimination against them. In recent years, indeed, attempts to combat by political means the results of their superior economic performance have become the cornerstone of official economic policy. (Other examples of the relative success of groups discriminated against are commonplace in economic history.) In Latin America also, the prosperity of the landowners, industrialists, and merchants has not been achieved at the expense of the poor. The economic conditions of the poorest groups, such as the Indians of Central and Southern America and the Negro descendants of slaves in Brazil, are no worse, and in many ways are far better, than were those of their ancestors. The economic conditions of Negroes in Brazil do not differ greatly from those of Africans in the more advanced parts of black Africa.

The notion that the incomes of the more prosperous have somehow been achieved at the expense of the less prosperous has had a long and disastrous history. In its duration and consequences it is perhaps the most pernicious of all economic misconceptions. On the contemporary scene it has contributed to the persecution of economically productive but politically unpopular and powerless minorities in the Third World.

There are, of course, major exceptions to the general proposition that the incomes of the prosperous are earned. Perhaps the most important exceptions are incomes derived predominantly from government-conferred privileges. Such privileges are especially significant and widespread in the extremely politicized societies of the Third World. Their many forms include state subsidies, restrictions on competition, allocations of licences, and privileged forms of employment. These privileged incomes are not what the Pope and other clerics have in mind in their attacks on inequality. Such privileged incomes are not relevant to international differences in income. And in the national sphere it is the papal view that governments act for the general good, so that the results of their policies cannot be the subject for redress through politically organized redistribution. Moreover, recipients of such privileged incomes are not necessarily rich. Finally, egalitarian discourse is addressed to income differences as such, not to privileged incomes *vis-à-vis* other incomes.[6]

6

Sometimes the papal documents do not ascribe the poverty of the poor to exploitation or oppression. Instead, the failure of poor people, notably poor societies, to share in contemporary prosperity is attributed to lack of natural resources, especially land.

Lack of natural resources, including land, has little or nothing to do with the poverty of individuals or of societies. Amidst abundant land and natural resources the American Indians before Columbus remained wretchedly poor when much of Europe with far less land was already rich. In the less developed world today, many millions of extremely poor people have abundant cultivable land. Over much of Asia, Africa, and Latin America very large numbers of extremely poor and backward people live in areas where cultivable but uncultivated land is free or extremely cheap. The small size and low productivity of farms and the presence of landless workers in such areas reflect not the shortage of land but primarily the lack of ambition, enterprise, and skill.

Of course, land which has been improved by the efforts and savings of productive people is the target for demands for redistribution even where unimproved land is plentiful. Who would not welcome a free gift of valuable assets? Land on its own is unproductive and yields nothing of value to mankind. It becomes productive as a result of ambition, perceptiveness, resourcefulness, and effort. These attributes and characteristics are present very unequally among different individuals, groups, and societies.

Sustained prosperity, as distinct from occasional windfalls, owes little or nothing to natural resources: witness West Germany, Switzerland, Japan, Singapore, Hong Kong, and Taiwan. The wide differences in economic performance between individuals and groups in the same country with access to the same natural resources throw into relief the personal and cultural differences behind economic achievement.

---

[6] Especially in the past, people have often acquired wealth not by peaceful economic contacts in commercial transactions, but by despoiling other people. Where there is no public security, the strong can despoil the weak so regularly that this is not even regarded as criminal. Such conditions may well have been widespread in the fourth century A.D. when St. Ambrose denounced the rich, though it is doubtful whether he specifically had in mind spoliation by the rich. The acquisition of wealth in this way does not, of course, represent the generation of income as this is usually understood. Moreover, spoliation results from lack of public security. Where a government fails to perform its primary function, it is extremely improbable that it would or could organize redistribution on any basis likely to be fair.

The conditions of the poorest and most backward people throughout the Third World, such as tribal societies, pygmies, and aborigines, cannot possibly have anything to do with lack of land, Western exploitation, or the activities of ethnic minorities.

These groups have few contacts either with the West or with economically active ethnic minorities. They also have abundant land at their disposal. Much the same applies to the causes of famine and to the lack of so-called basic facilities. For instance, the famines in sparsely populated African countries such as Ethiopia, the Sahel, Tanzania, Uganda, and Zaire reflect the low level of subsistence or near-subsistence activity, perpetuated or aggravated by the lack of public security and by damaging policies such as official suppression of trading activity, forced collectivization, and the persecution of productive groups, notably ethnic or tribal minorities.

7

Domestic and international redistribution are the overriding policy prescriptions in the papal documents. The former is to be effected by taxation or outright confiscation; the latter by politically organized government-to-government transfers of resources, known as foreign aid. I have questioned the case for domestic redistribution in section 5 above.[7] The economic, political, social, and moral implications of foreign aid are the subject of chapter 5 in this volume, and there is no need to traverse the same ground here. It is evident from chapter 5 that the papal documents ignore all the major issues involved in attempted global redistribution by means of foreign aid given to governments on the basis of the poverty of their subjects.

I turn now to some issues, including moral issues, raised by the Pope's general approach to income differences and to the policies appropriate to their reduction or elimination. This approach entails major spiritual and moral implications and consequences which many people may well consider even more destructive than the political and economic effects. I should perhaps recall here that the Pope's opinions expressed in *Populorum Progressio* and *Octogesima Adveniens* reflect what is virtually a consensus of opinions of contemporary clergy on what they call social justice. Indeed, the language of the younger Catholic clergy and of Protestant clergy is apt to be much more strident.

The persistent preoccupation with income differences and with the contrast in prosperity between the West and the Third World is much more likely to arouse envy than to elicit compassion. The allegations that pros-

---

[7] An extended discussion of redistribution within a country is in chapter 1 of Bauer, *Equality, the Third World and Economic Delusion*.

perity reflects misconduct and therefore injustice lace envy with resentment and righteous indignation. Such notions also reflect and reinforce the contemporary tendency to play down personal responsibility by suggesting that people's economic conditions depend on external forces rather than on themselves.

The modern clerical consensus endorsed by the Pope buttresses and encourages envy and resentment by conferring apparent moral legitimacy and intellectual validity on these sentiments. Insistence on politically organized redistribution within and between countries also fuels envy and resentment. Articulate clergymen and many academics have traditionally shared an attitude of suspicion and hostility towards people actively engaged in the process of wealth creation and also an attitude of supercilious disdain for its results.

Envy and resentment are soul-destroying sentiments liable to corrode people afflicted by them. What the Pope asserts, in common with so many other modern clergymen, serves to encourage one of the seven deadly sins.

To arouse these sentiments is to provoke tension and conflict. In this way conflicts originating in politicization or in other influences can be extended, intensified, and brutalized. Moreover, the fear of being exposed to envy and to its political and social consequences inhibits economic performance and improvement. This applies notably in tribal societies.

The catch-phrase "the earth belongs to all" epitomizes the central thrust of the papal documents and is bound to provoke envy, or something stronger. This slogan has become a rallying cry in inflammatory propaganda against the West and against well-to-do people both in the Third World and in the West. The principal theme is that some three-quarters of mankind languish in poverty, excluded from their rightful heritage through misconduct of the well-to-do and especially by the sinister domination of Western financial institutions and multinational companies.

A leaflet distributed in Chartres cathedral in 1979 is typical. Entitled (not surprisingly) "The Earth Belongs to All" (*Là terre est à tous*), the leaflet quotes a resolution of thirteen Brazilian bishops—who claim to be the voice of their voiceless people—that nothing will change in their country without fundamental changes in the advanced countries where the centres of domination and private capital are located. The leaflet insists that radical changes in the West are necessary to bring about a new international economic order, meaning large-scale confiscation of wealth as restitution for supposed economic wrongs. These political demands are described as the essence of Christ's message—the only mention of Christ in the four-page document.

Such propaganda plays upon and reinforces the widespread feeling of guilt in the West towards the Third World, a feeling which does nothing to assist the ordinary people in LDCs, but is more likely to harm them. Exponents of collective guilt rarely examine either the ground for their allegations or the results of the policies they propose. In the context of foreign aid, such allegations are most likely to lead to indiscriminate wealth transfers to Third World governments and to various international organizations. The emphasis on guilt precludes close examination either of conditions in the recipient countries or of the conduct of the recipient governments. These considerations are pertinent, especially because guilt so often parades as compassion and is so readily confused with it. The exponents of guilt routinely exempt themselves from their accusations; they do not speak of *mea culpa* but of *nostra culpa*, or rather *vestra culpa*. This is not accidental; allegations of collective guilt go hand in hand with a decline in personal responsibility and a sense of personal sin.

The Pope regards official transfers as a discharge of moral duty and as action substantially similar to voluntary charity. Yet there is an evident difference in moral content between voluntary sacrifice to help one's fellow men and public spending out of taxes. Taxpayers have no choice, and many may not know that they contribute for this particular purpose. The political and economic effects of the two forms of transfer also differ profoundly. The activities of voluntary agencies, especially nonpoliticized charities, do not politicize life as does official foreign aid, and thus they avoid the baleful results of the politicization of life promoted by official transfers. Moreover, voluntary charity is generally adjusted far more effectively to the conditions and needs of local people. In particular, voluntary agencies are much more interested in alleviating the lot of the poorest than are most rulers in the Third World.

At one point the Pope insists on liberating people from subjection to the forces of nature. But many millions of people in Asia do not share the Western outlook that nature should be harnessed to man's purposes. They think or feel that man should learn to live with nature rather than try to subordinate it to his own purposes. Generally, Western culture envisages nature as serving the purpose of man, who has the right, indeed the duty, to subordinate it to his own purposes. The indigenous cultures of South Asia envisage organic creation as a continuum which man has no special right to subject to his own purposes.

The Pope enjoins his audience to respect non-Western civilizations and cultures. The cultures of large parts of the less developed world are uncongenial to economic achievement and advance. The idea of material progress, in the sense of a steadily increasing control by man over nature, is wholly of Western origin. It is anomalous to insist that the West should respect Third World cultures and at the same time to urge that the West should pay taxes for the benefit of those who embrace cultures inimical to economic advance.

In the face of the clerical consensus on Western responsibility for Third World poverty, it was unexpected and refreshing recently to find an opinion by a Third World prelate who disagrees fundamentally with received opinion and who has the moral courage to say so. He is Monseigneur Bernard Bududira, bishop of Bururi in Burundi in Central Africa, and an African. Part of an article by the bishop in a French-language African journal was reproduced in German translation in the Swiss newspaper *Neue Zürcher Zeitung* of 4/5 January 1981. It is a remarkable article.

Bishop Bududira's principal theme is that the local cultures in Africa and elsewhere in the Third World obstruct material progress. The Bishop insists that economic improvement of a person depends on the person himself, notably on his mental attitudes and especially on his attitude to work. Unquestioning acceptance of nature and of its vagaries is widespread in Africa and elsewhere in the Third World. Man sees himself not as making history but as suffering it. To regard life as inexorably ordained by fate prevents a person from developing his or her potential. Under these influences people become passive rather than active, and the obligations of the extended family system stifle ambition and creative imagination. Initiative may be inhibited further by dependence upon tribal groups which suppress innovation and regard efforts for change and improvement as forms of rebellion. The Bishop concludes that the message of Christ frees people from the shackles of tribal thinking and leads to a greater sense of personal responsibility. The required changes can best be achieved by Christian groups working with local communities.

Some of these ideas used to be familiar, but they are very rarely heard nowadays. The translator commented that only an African could now write such an article. This observation is notable recognition of the success of the pedlars of Western guilt. Were it not for this factor, it would be by no means obvious why a European should not now write along such lines.

8

According to the opening paragraph of *Populorum Progressio,* the document is to help people "to grasp their serious problems in all its dimensions . . . at this turning point in human history." This promise is not fulfilled. The papal letters are not theological, doctrinal, or philosophical statements reaffirming Christian beliefs or helping people to find their bearings. They are political statements supported by bogus arguments, and as such can only confuse believers.

As will be clear from what has gone before, the Pope has lost all contact with reality, in both what he says and what he ignores. Amidst large-scale civil conflict (as in Nigeria and Vietnam at the time of *Populorum Progressio*), massacres, mass persecution, and expulsions in LDCs, the Pope wrote about the solidarity and brotherhood of humanity in the less developed world and also stated that governments always act for the common good. He ignores the relation between culture and economic achievement and the relevance of mores and beliefs to economic performance and progress. There is also a complete disregard of historical processes and of the perspective of time, as evidenced by the neglect of the fact that until very recently extreme material backwardness characterized most of the Third World. And yet applications of the time perspective used to be very much an element in Catholic thinking.

Even the eternal verities are overlooked. The responsibility of a person for the consequences of his actions and the fundamental distinction between mankind and the rest of creation are basic Christian tenets. They are pertinent to the issues raised by the Pope; but they are ignored throughout these documents.

In common with many other modern Christian clerics, Paul VI, his predecessor John XXIII, and to some extent also John Paul II, have chosen to speak on subjects with which they have been unfamiliar. People who pronounce on matters about which they are ignorant are apt simply to absorb ideas propagated or taken up by other élite or establishment groups. Nature abhors a vacuum not only in the physical world but also in the world of politics and ideas.

The Pope's arguments and allegations reflect unthinking surrender to intellectual fashion and political nostrums. This is obvious in the major themes, particularly in the insistence on large-scale official aid. The more specific topics and proposals are also a recital of modish remedies such as land reform, debt cancellation, commodity agreements and regional cooperation among LDCs.

The spirit of these documents is contrary to the most durable and best elements in Catholic tradition. They are indeed even unChristian. Their Utopian, chiliastic ideology, combined with an overriding preoccupation with economic differences, is an amalgam of the ideas of millenarian sects, of the extravagant claims of the early American advocates of foreign aid, and of the Messianic component of Marxism-Leninism.

There is a familiar and ominous ring in the insistence that economic advance requires "bold transformations, innovations that go deep" by political means. Such a stance has been regularly advanced to justify pervasive coercion and brutal policies. These harsh consequences are a familiar outcome of replacing conduct based on experience and reflection by ideological politics. In this sphere also it is true that those who wish to turn men into angels are more likely to turn them into beasts. The chiliasm of these documents is alien to the traditional down-to-earth attitude of the Catholic Church in worldly matters.

Populorum Progressio and *Octogesima Adveniens* are documents which are immoral on several levels. To begin with they are incompetent, and they are immoral because they are incompetent. Their lack of reflection and ideological commitment leads to proposals and promotes policies directly at variance with the declared sentiments and objectives of the papal documents. There is profound truth in Pascal's maxim that working hard to think clearly is the beginning of moral conduct. This applies with altogether special force to the head of a worldwide Church issuing major pronouncements. The documents are also immoral in that they give colour to the notion that envy can be legitimate; and they spread confusion about the meaning of charity.

It seems that many contemporary churchmen have lost their way and have moved into realms which are strange to them. They may perhaps have been seeking a new role for themselves in the face of widespread erosion or even the collapse of traditional beliefs. Their preoccupations may reflect a panic reaction to fear of the loss of their clientele. Some of the utterances of the modern clergy recall Othello's predicament when he felt that his occupation had gone, together with the attendant pomp and circumstance. It is paradoxical that the clergy are preoccupied with material conditions and progress at a time when the failure of material prosperity and advance to secure happiness, satisfaction, and tranquillity is everywhere evident.

Acceptance of ideas plainly at variance with reality may, however, also reflect the ready credulity of people, clerics included, who have lost their faith. Chesterton predicted long ago that when men cease to believe in a deity, they do not believe in nothing: they then simply believe in anything.

Truth may be great and will perhaps prevail. Scholars at any rate must act as if they believed both parts of this statement. But it requires exceptional strength of belief to hope that truth will triumph in the decades ahead in egalitarian discussions, especially about the Third World. The modern clerical consensus will certainly not help it to victory. Prelates such as Bishop Bududira might do so.

IX

Hong Kong

HOW WOULD you rate the economic prospects of an Asian country which has very little land (and only eroded hillsides at that) and which is indeed the most densely populated country in the world; whose population has grown rapidly, both through natural increase and large-scale immigration; which imports all its oil and raw materials and even most of its water; whose government is not engaged in development planning and operates no exchange controls or restrictions on capital exports and imports; and which is the only remaining Western colony of any significance?[1] You would think that this country must be doomed, unless it received large external donations. Or rather you would have to believe this, if you went by what politicians of all parties, the UN and its affiliates, prominent economists, and the quality press all say about less developed countries. Has not the vicious circle of poverty, the idea that poverty is self-perpetuating, been a cornerstone of mainstream development economics since World War II, and has it not been explicitly endorsed by Nobel Laureates Gunnar Myrdal and Paul Samuelson? Have not the development economists of the Massachusetts Institute of Technology said categorically about less developed countries that

> The general scarcity relative to population of nearly all resources creates a self-perpetuating vicious circle of poverty. Additional capital is necessary to increase output, but poverty itself makes it impossible to carry out the required saving and investment by a voluntary reduction in consumption.[2]

Has not Gunnar Myrdal insisted that "there must be something wrong with an underdeveloped country that does not have foreign exchange difficulties"? Did he not also say that all development experts agreed that comprehensive planning was the first condition of economic progress, and, indeed has this not been the opinion of the most prominent development economists in recent decades? Again, did not the celebrated Pearson Report, commissioned by the World Bank, say that "no other phenomenon casts a darker shadow over the prospects of international development than the

This essay is an extended version of that originally published in the *London Spectator* 224 (19 April 1980).

[1] In 1997 Britain gave over Hong Kong to China.

[2] *Study submitted by the Center for International Studies of the Massachusetts Institute of Technology to the Senate Committee investigating the operation of Foreign Aid* (Washington, D.C.: Government Printing Office, 1957), p. 37.

staggering growth of population"? And, finally, did not the United Nations Conference on Trade and Development (UNCTAD) enshrine in its General Principle Fourteen that "the liquidation of the remnants of colonialism in all its forms is a necessary condition of economic development"?

Thus according to the emphatic view of the most respected academic figures in the field, and of representatives of so-called world opinion, even one of the half a dozen characteristics with which I began would ensure persistent poverty.

But if instead of following fashion, you think for yourself and go by obvious evidence, then you will know that Hong Kong, the country in question, has progressed phenomenally since the 1940s, when it was still very poor, and that it has become such a formidable competitor that the leading Western countries erect barriers against its exports to protect their own domestic industries against this distant country. If you enquired further, you would know that incomes and real wages have risen rapidly in Hong Kong in recent decades. And incidentally Hong Kong is only an extreme case of a more general phenomenon because somewhat similar though less pronounced material progress has occurred in a number of countries or areas—South Korea, Taiwan, Singapore among them—when according to the experts this should have been impossible.

If you suspected all along that the established opinion on these matters was patently unfounded, you will welcome a short but instructive monograph, *Hong Kong: A Study in Economic Freedom* (University of Chicago Press) by Dr. Alvin Rabushka. Rabushka, an American political scientist turned economist, knows Hong Kong well, and his wife is Chinese. He has an incisive mind. He writes clearly, confidently, and indeed with gusto. His principal themes are not difficult, though it needs a firm mind and some courage to set them out so concisely and vigorously.

Rabushka reviews the processes and methods by which in less than 140 years, a few empty barren rocks grew into a major industrial trading and financial centre of about five million people. He ascribes this economic success story to the aptitudes of the people and to the pursuit of appropriate policies. Enterprise, hard work, ability to spot and utilise economic opportunities, are widespread in a population 98 percent Chinese, engaged in singleminded pursuit of making money day and night. Many are immigrants who brought skills and enterprise mostly from China, especially Shanghai, erstwhile centre of skill and enterprise of mainland China. The policies emphasised by Rabushka are fiscal conservatism; low taxation; the charging of market prices for specific government services; liberal immigration policy, at least until recently; free trade in both directions; unrestricted movement of capital into and out of the country; minimal government involvement in commercial life, including refusal to grant privileges to sectional interests. There are no special incentives or barriers to foreign investment, no insistence on local participation in foreign-owned enterprises. There are also no tax holidays or other special concessions to foreign investment, but equally there are no restrictions on the withdrawal of capital or on the remission of profits. These liberal policies, notably the freedom to withdraw capital, were designed to encourage the inflow of productive capital and enterprise, which indeed they did.

The lack of natural resources together with colonial rule encouraged both official economic nonintervention and fiscal conservatism. Absence of natural resources has encouraged an open economy with a large volume of exports to pay for the necessary imports. Such an economy requires a wide range of competitive exports and also competitive domestic markets. Government assistance to particular economic activities diverts resources from more productive uses and undermines the international competitive position of the economy. Moreover, in an economy as open as Hong Kong, the wasteful results of such subsidies become apparent sooner than elsewhere. Thus the very absence of natural resources has assisted material progress by discouraging wasteful policies. Inappropriate policies are much more likely to inhibit economic advance than does a lack of physical resources. Sustained budget deficits financed by credit creation also tend to bring about wasteful spending, so that poverty of resources discourages deficit finance. In the traditional British colonial accounting system, colonies could not run sustained budget deficits, and this tradition was continued after fiscal autonomy in 1958, partly for the reasons just noted. The absence of election promises, together with an open economy and limited government, have much reduced the prizes of political activity and therefore interest in organising pressure groups. All this encouraged fiscal conservatism—that is, low taxation, balanced budgets, and the charging of market prices for specific public services. The wish to attract foreign capital, the business outlook of a traditional trading community, and the general preoccupation with moneymaking also worked in this direction.

The official policies and the aptitudes and habits of the population have brought about an economy capable of rapid adjustment. This adaptability has enabled Hong Kong to survive and even to prosper in the face of numerous restrictions against its exports, often imposed or increased at short notice.

For social reasons, the principle of charging market prices for specific government services has for some time been subject to major exceptions. Large-scale provision of subsidised housing for the poor and the rationing of water by cutting off supplies for certain periods, rather than by charging higher prices for a continuous supply, are the two most important exceptions. They were introduced after much heart-searching and with an eye on local social conditions. The subsidies are moreover largely confined to the really poor. In addition to these subsidies in kind, there are substantial cash subsidies to the poor to ensure minimum incomes, and there are also various disability and infirmity grants. Comprehensive compulsory primary education, in fact as well as in name, and extensive public health services, have operated for many years.

In recent years Hong Kong has come to be much pressed both by the British government and by various international bodies to move towards a fully fledged so-called welfare state, complete with trade union privileges, comprehensive social services, far-reaching labour legislation, and redistributive taxation. Rabushka rightly notes that these external pressures reflect mainly a wish to serve various Western interests, as for instance by reducing competition from Hong Kong by inflating costs there. Rabushka also refers to the unease or even resentment engendered in the supporters of state-controlled economies by the rapid rise in general living standards in this and other market-oriented economies. These external pressures may yet gain support within Hong Kong from ambitious administrators, discontented intellectuals, and aspiring politicians, all of whom hope for greater scope in a more politicised society. Governor Sir Murray McLehose is also more concerned with external opinion than were his predecessors. Rabushka believes, I think rightly, that the expiry in 1997 of the lease of much of the territory of Hong Kong from China, or possible hostile action from the People's Republic of China, are less of a menace to the future of Hong Kong than trade barriers in the West and Western pressures for the introduction of further labour legislation, a comprehensive welfare state, and other policies which inflate costs and reduce adaptability.

Rabushka's unashamed admiration for Hong Kong and for its market economy pervades the book.

> Dare I reveal my boorishness by saying that I find Hong Kong's economic hustle and bustle more interesting, entertaining, and liberating than its lack of high opera, music, and drama? East has indeed met West in the market economy. Chinese and Europeans in Hong Kong have no time for racial quarrels, which would only interfere with making money. This prospect of individual gain in the marketplace makes group activity for political gain unnecessary—the market economy is truly color-blind. (p. 85)

There is some oversimplification here. For instance, pursuit of moneymaking can readily go together with racial strife in state-controlled economies. The crucial factor is not moneymaking as such but limited government. It is, however, clear that a society such as Hong Kong offers little scope for the ambitious literati, who often become disgruntled or even hostile. Until recently at any rate, the economic philosophy of the government offered few employment opportunities for social scientists, especially economists. No official estimates of the national income were published before 1973. This in no way inhibited a spectacular rise in incomes and living standards. But it reduced the employment opportunities of economists, statisticians, and civil servants and thus of university graduates, which again aroused hostility among the literati at home and abroad.

Apart from the main themes, there is much informative and unexpected detail in this book. For instance, who would have thought that in 1843 the British foreign secretary insisted that if as a result of the creation of a free port "many people were attracted to Hong Kong, then H.M. Government would feel justified in securing to the Crown the increased values that the land would then have."

The decisive role in economic life of personal aptitudes and motivations, social mores, and of appropriate political arrangements is the outstanding lesson of Hong Kong. Access to markets is also important, but less fundamental. Other countries also have had access to outside markets and supplies, without producing such an economic success story. Physical or financial resources are much less important, or even insignificant, compared to personal and social factors and appropriate political arrangements, especially firm but limited government.

The notion that low income sets up a vicious circle of poverty and stagnation confuses poverty with its causes. To have money is the result of economic achievement, not its precondition. The utilisation of natural resources depends entirely on the other factors just noted. In certain market conditions or political situations, the possession or acquisition of natural resources can bring windfalls, even large windfalls; witness the gold and silver of the Americas in the sixteenth century and the operations of OPEC in the twentieth century. But hitherto at any rate, such windfalls have not led to lasting economic progress, much less to such sustained and spectacular advance as that of Hong Kong. Nor is economic success without natural resources anything new, as is evident for instance from Venice, the Low Countries, Switzerland, and Japan. Conversely, backwardness amidst large natural resources is evident from the American Indians to the present Third World, where many millions of extremely backward people live amidst unlimited cultivable land. Well over one hundred years ago de Tocqueville wrote,

> Looking at the turn given to the human spirit in England by political life; seeing the Englishman, certain of the support of his laws, relying on himself and unaware of any obstacle except the limit of his own powers, acting without constraint . . . I am in no hurry to inquire whether nature has scooped out ports for him, and given him coal and iron. The reason for his commercial prosperity is not there at all: it is in himself.[3]

[3] Alexis de Tocqueville, *Journeys to England and Ireland,* (1833), ed. J. P. Mayer (London: Faber and Faber, 1958).

Hong Kong bears out that population increase is not an obstacle to progress, that suitably motivated people are assets not liabilities, agents of progress as well as its beneficiaries. It shows also that economic performance owes little to formal education. In Hong Kong as elsewhere in the Far East, the economic performance or success of hundreds of thousands or even millions of people has resulted not from formal education, but from industry, enterprise, thrift, and ability to use economic opportunity. This is disturbing to professional educationalists, who like to market their wares as necessary for economic achievement.

Other lessons from Hong Kong are again discernible elsewhere but stand out especially clearly there. Hong Kong is yet another evident refutation of the staples of the dominant, mainstream development literature which I have mentioned earlier, such as that poverty must be self-perpetuating; that balance of payments difficulties are inevitable in economic advance from poverty; that comprehensive planning and foreign aid are indispensable or even sufficient for economic progress. Yet these fables are propagated throughout the West by the international organisations, by aid agencies, and by academics financed by taxpayers and by the large foundations. Indeed the propagators of these myths command almost unlimited resources which makes it more difficult to expose their fables. Hong Kong experience offends respectable opinion in other ways also. It shows that planning teams and advisory groups are unnecessary for development; and by contrast with the experience of other countries, groaning under the policies advocated by the United Nations and by mainstream academic advisors, it shows that their activities are likely to be damaging. Hong Kong has unforgivably succeeded in defiance of the best professional opinion.

Hong Kong is unpopular with the aid lobbies and the politicised charities. These groups are hostile to people who can dispense with their ministrations. Hence the bad press which Hong Kong has in the West and the hostility it encounters from the great and the good. The achievement is ignored or underplayed, and the shortcomings, whether real or alleged, avoidable or inevitable, are prominently featured. Overcrowding and child labour are examples. In all these respects Hong Kong compares very favourably with the rest of Asia. For instance, real wages are the highest in Asia, except for Japan. But if a government tries to run a socialist economy, or at any rate a largely state-controlled one, Western politicians, writers, academics, and journalists are apt to present hardship or even suffering there as inevitable or even commend it as the result of laudable efforts to promote progress. But if the government relies on a market economy, then any deviation from arbitrary and Western-inspired norms is regarded as a defect or even a crime. And if in addition such a country is successful and also dispenses with official aid or politicised charity, the conduct of the government or even of the population will be regarded as objectionable.

According to UNCTAD General Principle Fourteen, colonial status is incompatible with material progress. This was formally announced in 1964, years after Hong Kong had been progressing rapidly and when the inroads of Hong Kong products in Western markets caused much embarrassment. Whatever one thinks about Western colonialism, UNCTAD General Principle Fourteen is a self-evident untruth. This is clear not only from Hong Kong but also from the large-scale advance of many Western colonies, including Malaysia, Nigeria, the Gold Coast, the Ivory Coast, and Singapore. Yet this patent untruth was solemnly announced at a major international conference largely financed by the West.

Another implication of the Hong Kong experience also straddles politics and the intellectual climate. Whether a country is a colony or an independent sovereign state has nothing to do with personal freedom there. The newly independent African states are habitually termed free, meaning that their governments are sovereign. But the people there are far from free, less free than they were under colonial rule. They are certainly much less free than people are in Hong Kong. Hong Kong is a dictatorship, in that people do not have the vote. But in their personal life, especially their economic life, they are far freer than most people in the West. Hong Kong should remind us that in the modern world a nonelective government can be more limited than an elected one and that, for most ordinary people, it is arguably more important whether government is limited or unlimited than whether it is elective or nonelective.

Effective Influence on Opinion:
The Shenoy Memorial Lecture

B. R. Shenoy was a hero and a saint. He was a hero in the sense in which Thomas Sowell used the term when in a review article he referred to heroic figures who publicly resisted fashionable fads and fancies, however influentially canvassed and widely accepted. He was a saint in that, outwardly at any rate, he remained unmoved, even serene, in the face of neglect, disparagement, even abuse. It is an honor to lecture in memory of such a man. For me it is also an emotional experience. I knew Shenoy personally and felt great affection and respect for him. I had several extended conversations with him in the late 1950s when he was particularly embattled.

In this lecture I shall quote at length not from Shenoy but from publications reflecting the received opinion, amounting to an orthodoxy, in the 1950s and 1960s both in India and in mainstream development economics in the West. Unless I quote from this literature I cannot convey the difficulties and obstacles Shenoy had to face. And unless I quote at considerable length and from several sources some may think that the passages are out of context or are unrepresentative.

COMPREHENSIVE ECONOMIC PLANNING: SHENOY'S DISSENT

I had never heard of Shenoy until I read the literature surrounding the Indian Second Five Year Plan launched in 1956. I first encountered his name as that of the author of his one-man Note of Dissent (Shenoy 1955), appended to the Majority Report of the government advisory panel of economists on the draft of the Second Five Year Plan. The government then had a panel of some twenty economists who in April 1955 submitted to the government the draft for an ambitious development plan. This draft in turn drew heavily on a draft plan entitled Draft Plan Frame by Professor P. C. Mahalanobis, Nehru's personal economic adviser. The Majority Report and Mahalanobis's Draft Plan Frame formed the basis of the Second Five Year Plan, the text of which was published by the Government Planning Commission in 1956.

Cato Journal 18, no. 1 (Spring/Summer 1998). Copyright © Cato Institute. All rights reserved. This article is a slightly revised version of the Prof. B. R. Shenoy Memorial Lecture, which was delivered in Ahmedabad, Gujarat, in March 1993.

These various documents all took for granted that comprehensive central planning was indispensable for economic progress. They envisaged large-scale money creation for the financing of the highly ambitious Second Five Year Plan, maintenance and expansion of a wide range of economic controls, and extensive nationalization. In his Note of Dissent, Shenoy rejected the general spirit of the Majority Report as endangering personal freedom and a democratic political system. He also disagreed with several major proposals, including the scale of money creation, the maintenance and extension of state economic controls, and the scope of nationalization. He argued specifically that money creation on the scale envisaged by the Majority Report and under the Second Five Year Plan would result in inflation or a balance of payments crisis or both—a prediction that was fulfilled barely a year after the inception of the plan. Both the spirit of the Majority Report and the major proposals reflected the opinions of Nehru, who was then at the peak of his power in India and of his prestige there and in the West. In these conditions, Shenoy's Note of Dissent represented conspicuous moral courage. Moreover, Mahalanobis's Draft Plan Frame and the Second Five Year Plan very largely reflected the then-dominant opinion of development economics in the West. Thus, Shenoy's Note of Dissent went counter to the opinions and wishes of Nehru and his personal adviser and also of the position of the Indian Planning Commission. It also went counter to the then-current orthodoxy in the West. Many prominent representatives of that orthodoxy regularly visited India in the 1950s and 1960s. The visitors included Gunnar Myrdal, Joan Robinson, Nicholas Kaldor, Thomas Balogh, Ian Little, Oscar Lange, Paul Streeten, and others. Most of these representatives of the prevailing orthodoxy endorsed the Second Five Year Plan in public pronouncements in India and in prestigious and influential publications in the West, such as the *Economic Journal* or the *Review* of the British National Institute for Economic Research.

The great majority of the representatives of the official national and international aid agencies were committed supporters of the orthodoxy, as were the representatives in India of the Ford Foundation, then the principal source of unofficial aid, whose representatives worked closely with the Planning Commission. Thus, Shenoy's position also went counter to the opinions of people who very largely determined the allocation and disbursement of Western aid. Here are two examples of the position of these representatives.

On my first visit to India in 1958, I called on a senior officer of the economic section of the British High Commission. I asked him whether he or his colleagues were in any sort of contact with Shenoy. He said that people there were too busy to have time for acknowledged madmen. It also transpired that he was unfamiliar with the writings or even existence of British or American dissenters from the prevailing orthodoxy. I may add that at about the same time I visited the Delhi School of Economics and the National Council of Applied Economic Research. There also I found considerable and often not well-founded disagreement with Shenoy's views, but nothing like the disdain exhibited by this arrogant and ignorant mandarin at the High Commission.

My second example is from an American source. In 1962, John P. Lewis, a full professor of economics at Princeton University and director of the Indian operation of the U.S. Agency for International Development (the official U.S. aid agency), published a substantial volume entitled *Quiet Crisis in India*. Here is a passage from that book:

> It has been decided in India that it is the duty of government—and it cannot be delegated—to create and maintain that "growth perspective" which . . . is the one *sine qua non* for successful economic development.
>
> Outside supporters of the Indian development program who refuse to accept this proposition well-nigh disqualify themselves from the outset. (Lewis 1962, p. 28)

Although this passage is convoluted, the central thrust is clear. Those who dispute the necessity of government control of the composition and direction of economic activity are not qualified to participate in the shaping of economic policy. Thus, according to the director of the most important aid agency then operating in India, Shenoy's position disqualified him from a say in policy. I do not know how much comfort he drew from the fact that he shared this disqualification with Milton Friedman, George Stigler, Gottfried Haberler, Jacob Viner, and others.

Lewis's opinion was not eccentric. Indeed, it largely reflected the received opinion of the 1950s and 1960s. Gunnar Myrdal expressed substantially the same opinion in his much publicized Cairo lectures:

> The alternative to making the heroic attempt is continued acquiescence in economic and cultural stagnation or regression which is politically impossible in the world of today; and this is, of course, the explanation why grand scale national planning is at present the goal in underdeveloped countries all over the globe and why this policy line is unanimously endorsed by governments and experts in the advanced countries. (Myrdal 1956b, p. 65)

Thus, according to Myrdal, experts were unanimous in the 1950s that comprehensive central planning was indispensable for the economic advance of poor countries. It followed that those who like Shenoy disputed this view could not be experts, whatever their formal qualifications, technical competence, or knowledge of the institutional setting.

I trust that I have conveyed something of Shenoy's moral courage in dissenting from the Second Five Year Plan and the orthodoxy surrounding it. But dissent from the received opinion is by itself of no merit unless it is intellectually well founded. Shenoy amply met this requirement. His competence is not in dispute. The tools of trade of economists acting as advisers on policy are microeconomics, macroeconomics (or applied monetary economics and public finance), and knowledge of institutions and magnitudes. Shenoy qualified under all these headings. I commend his Note of Dissent and his book *Problems of Indian Economic Development* (Shenoy 1958) as highly informative introductions to applied monetary economics and to political economy. These publications are not easily accessible, but the effort is worthwhile.

Shenoy's Note of Dissent does not readily lend itself to brief summary or quotation, chiefly because much of it refers to contemporary statistical evidence in support of his position or to the Majority Report and to documents underlying it. However, the following passages from the Note of Dissent (Shenoy 1955, pp. 25, 30) make clear his general position:

> The size of the Plan Frame has been unduly inflated as a result, on the one hand, of an over-optimistic growth in national income, which it aims at, and, on the other, of an unduly high average rate of saving as applied to this assumed growth in income. A much lower figure would result if both these rates were more realistic projections of Indian experience of the recent past. Though a certain measure of accelerated progress may result as incomes grow and savings increase, a steep upward movement from a background in which the mass of the people live on the margin of subsistence may not be possible except in a totalitarian regime.

> I agree with my colleagues that the scarcity of administrative and specialized personnel, and the necessity of conserving savings for the Plan are factors against extension of nationalization. But they have no objection for such extension on principle. I would oppose general extension of nationalization on principle. Nationalization should be ordinarily limited to public utility concerns and to concerns involving national security. Otherwise state intervention should be concerned with the prevention of monopolies or quasimonopolies. Efficient management of business and industrial concerns in a competitive market economy is a highly specialized function and demands qualities which a civil servant is not required to, and in the ordinary course of his training may not, acquire. This function is best left to private entrepreneurs, in the prevailing socioeconomic order which is dominated by the market economy and the pricing system.

> I do not feel convinced of the economic importance of continuing the remnants of controls. Decontrols have proved a noteworthy success. Controls and physical allocations are not a necessary adjunct to planning. The distribution of productive resources, including the ratios in which they are used, are subject to variation and depend upon diverse technological, economic and price considerations. It is quite impossible to take into account these complex and changing considerations and arrange anything like a satisfactory allocation of resources. There are great advantages in allowing freedom to the economy,

and to the price system in the use and distribution of the needs of production. I am unable to agree with my colleagues that a case exists for continuing what controls now remain. Steps should be taken to remove controls as early as may be possible. Controls and allocations are an essential characteristic of communist planning. They do not very well fit in under planning in a free enterprise market economy.

THE MID-1950S: HIGH WATER MARK OF PRICE-LESS AND COST-LESS ECONOMICS

In contrast to Shenoy's assured command of basic price theory and basic monetary economics, influential publication in India and the West of the orthodoxy reflects notable, even startling, neglect both of the basic tenets of economics and of simple empirical evidence.

The mid-1950s—that is, the period of the preparation and launching of the Second Five Year Plan—were the high water mark of price-less and cost-less economics (i.e., disregard of price in discussion of supply and demand, or more precisely, in quantities demanded or supplied). It was in the 1950s that prominent academic economists discussed the so-called dollar problem as a persistent and inescapable shortage of dollars, without mentioning the rate of exchange (i.e., the price of a scarce commodity), or for that matter interest rates either. From the dollar problem, this practice spread to the payment difficulties of less developed countries (LDCs). Exponents of the orthodoxy regarded these difficulties as inseparable concomitants of the economic progress of LDCs and especially of government policies designed to permit it. In reality, they were the consequences of inflationary policies pursued under conditions of fixed exchange rates, as was recognized by Shenoy. Gunnar Myrdal, perhaps the most prominent and influential Western guru in India, went as far as writing that "there must be something wrong with an underdeveloped country that does not have foreign exchange difficulties" (Myrdal 1956a, p. 270).

This totally and demonstrably unfounded opinion suited the purposes of the proponents of ambitious plans financed in part by large-scale money creation.

INDIA'S SECOND FIVE YEAR PLAN AND THE WORLD BANK REPORT

Let me now present two specific and detailed pronouncements of the orthodoxy of the mid-1950s. First, a central passage from the Indian Second Five Year Plan:

The expansion of the iron and steel industry has obviously been the highest priority since, more than any other industrial product, the levels of production in these materials determine the tempo of progress of the economy as a whole. . . . Heavy engineering industries are a natural corollary of iron and steel works. . . . In this context the creation of basic facilities such as the establishment of heavy foundries, forges and structural shops is absolutely necessary. It is, therefore, proposed that the establishment of these facilities, which constitute an essential and primary phase of development for the manufacture of heavy industrial machinery in the country, should be undertaken at an early date. These developments have a priority second only to that of expansion of the steel industry. (Government of India Planning Commission 1956, p. 394)

These remarks reflect price-less economics; neither price nor cost nor demand is mentioned.

My second example comes from a World Bank report. In 1955, the World Bank published a long report of its mission to Nigeria, which it considered as a guide to policy and as a model for this kind of document. The principal architect of the report was John H. Adler, who had taught at Yale, and who subsequently became the director of the World Bank Economic Development Institute, a prestigious organization for the training of development economists.

Throughout the report the influence of prices on quantities demanded, supplied, or produced is neglected. Demand and supply are treated as physical quantities affected by various factors, but not by price:

Expansion [of agriculture] in the immediate future and over the long term will depend upon the degree to which Nigeria can succeed in overcoming or minimizing the effect of such limiting factors as soil deficiencies, inadequacy of water supply in certain areas, low yielding plant varieties, prevalence of plant and livestock diseases, and primitive cultivation methods. (World Bank 1955, p. 371)

Thus, price is not listed among the factors influencing production or the establishment of capacity.

In this case the neglect of price was especially inappropriate. The report was intended as a guide to policy. The producer prices of the principal crops were prescribed by state buying monopolies. And because of large distances and heavy transport costs, the wide extensive margin of cultivation between cash crops and subsistence production, and the ability of producers to shift between activities and crops, the supply of farm products and extension of capacity necessarily depended upon price. Production was possible only with a positive return, and the area in which it was positive depended upon price. Neglect of price necessarily vitiated proposals for an effective fiscal policy.

The Indian Second Five Year Plan and the World Bank report on Nigeria were perhaps the two most important official documents influencing policy in LDCs in the 1950s. They show how price-less economics had engulfed development economics in the 1950s. This development much enhanced the difficulties of Shenoy's stance as he was a market-oriented economist with an assured command of applied basic price theory.

THE DANGER OF EXTERNAL ECONOMIC ADVICE

I said earlier that I had never heard of Shenoy before reading the literature of the Second Five Year Plan. Yet I had heard of several other members of the Government's Advisory Panel, notably D. R. Gadgil, B. N. Ganguli, K. N. Raj, and V. K. R. V. Rao. This reflected the much closer international contacts between socialists or dirigistes on one hand and market-oriented economists on the other hand, a situation to which F. A. Hayek drew attention many years ago. The overwhelming preponderance of supporters of the Second Five Year Plan among foreign visitors to India, including consultants to the government, also reflected this phenomenon, which exacerbated the difficulties of Shenoy in securing acceptance for his views.

There is an important practical lesson to be learned from this experience. Why should the Indian government or its offshoots and agencies rely on external economic advice? The tools of trade of an adviser on economic policy are microeconomic theory, macroeconomic theory (primarily applied monetary economics and public finance), and a knowledge of institutions and magnitudes. There is in India ample indigenous talent in analytical and applied economics. In recent years Indians have occupied some of the most prestigious university chairs in economics at Oxford, Cambridge, the London School of Economics, Harvard, Yale, and the University of California. And, of course, Indians are likely to have a far better knowledge of institutions and magnitudes than have foreigners. If an Indian government uses external advisers, it should recognize that the advisers are likely to be people whose advice will be in the direction of the maintenance or expansion of the role of the institutions sponsoring them. The government may wish for political reasons to rely on such external advisers, especially if it thinks that by doing so it is more likely to secure external financial support. But the government should be aware of the substantive direction of the advice, which may often differ from the lip service paid by the advisers to the market and to traditional institutions.

SHENOY'S INFLUENCE

Shenoy has had no influence on Indian economic policy. The original Second Five Year Plan and its various subsequent revisions and sequels reflected the play of political forces and the recurrent balance of payment crises. I believe however that he had considerable impact on the conduct and thinking of Indian economists younger than himself.

This opinion is necessarily conjectural. People's views on economic issues are affected by a multitude of different factors operating with differing and varying time lags. One is prone to overstate the influence of those economists whose views one favors. And economists are apt to make unwarranted claims for the profession. In an often-quoted passage Keynes (1936, p. 383) wrote, "The ideas of economists and political philosophers both when they are right, and when they are wrong, are more powerful than is commonly understood. Indeed, the world is ruled by little else." If this claim were valid, the world would have been on free trade for decades or centuries, as the great majority of economists have been free traders since Adam Smith.

I can however say with some confidence that Shenoy's conduct and influence have had considerable impact. In the course of my visits to India between 1958 and 1982, a number of economists, including M. P. Bhatt, told me that they had been influenced by Shenoy in that they revised their opinions or have become more confident in their position through reading his work.

There is certainly one economist of whom I can say with absolute confidence that he was influenced by Shenoy. This is myself. He has influenced both my conduct and my opinions. And as it appears from my correspondence that I have influenced some younger people, often in distant countries, Shenoy's impact has extended beyond myself.

The contrast between Shenoy's lack of influence on policy and his impact on other economists is an example of a widely prevalent situation. The political unacceptability or unpopularity of an opinion does not mean that its proponent is less influential than are those whose views are more readily accepted. These latter are sometimes known as realists. There is often a high correlation between the advice tendered by economists and the policy adopted without this indicating that the advisers exercise influence in any meaningful sense. They may only advise policymakers to do what the latter intend to do in any case. Indeed, they may have been selected as advisers because the policymakers anticipated that they would tender the kind of advice which makes it easier for the policymakers to carry out policies and measures which they had planned. I think this was the situation in India at the time of the Second Five Year Plan. The signatories of the Majority Report appeared to be influential since the plan accorded with their views. In reality, they simply endorsed what the government of the day wished to do in any case. So they had little influence either on thought or on policy. In contrast Shenoy's conduct and views influenced a number of people in India and beyond.

CONCLUSION

It is evident from what I have said that Shenoy united moral courage, intellectual integrity, and technical competence to an exceptional degree. The few people who possess this combination of attributes are of great value, both in public life and in academic study. They are particularly valuable in the study of society, where they are especially rare. May the succession of Shenoy and of his like never fail, East or West.

REFERENCES

Government of India. Planning Commission. 1956. *Second Five Year Plan*. Delhi: Government of India Planning Commission.

Keynes, J. M. 1936. *The General Theory of Employment, Interest, and Money*. London: Macmillan.

Lewis, J. P. 1962. *Quiet Crisis in India: Economic Development and American Policy*. Washington, D.C.: Brookings Institution.

Myrdal, G. 1956a. *An International Economy: Problems and Prospects*. London: Routledge and Kegan Paul.

———. 1956b. *Development and Underdevelopment*. Cairo: National Bank of Egypt.

Shenoy, B. R. 1955. Note of Dissent. In *Papers Relating to the Formulation of the Second Five Year Plan*. Delhi: Government of India Planning Commission.

———. 1958. *Problems of Indian Economic Development*. Madras: University of Madras Press.

World Bank. 1955. *The Economic Development of Nigeria* [report of a mission organized by the International Bank for reconstruction and development at the request of the governments of Nigeria and the United Kingdom]. Baltimore: Johns Hopkins University Press.

Class on the Brain

THE STANDARD CLICHÉ

IN THE 1970s, when Herr Schmidt was the West German chancellor, he provided a terse summary of received opinion on the subject of class. He was on an official visit to London in December 1975 when the pound was weak and the balance of payments in heavy deficit. He was reported in the *Financial Times* as saying:

> As long as you maintain that damned class-ridden society of yours you will never get out of your mess.[1]

And indeed this was what foreigners are told all the time by the British intelligentsia. Thus the *Financial Times'* staff writer, who quoted Herr Schmidt approvingly, went on to say:

> The single most important fault in Britain's social structure remains its propensity to accentuate class differences. . . . Most foreigners can see this, but many people in Britain are curiously blind to the grim reality behind the Chancellor's words.

This is part of a stereotype. For many years now, politicians, journalists, and academics have blamed on the class system just about every form of economic adversity or social malaise in Britain. Some of these allegations are plainly far-fetched as, for example, the idea that a weak pound reflects the class system; they do not often say the converse when the pound is strong. Thus, speaking again in London in October 1977, Herr Schmidt said that the British economy had improved greatly; but on that occasion he said nothing about class.

In spite of the mounting academic evidence (which as we shall see, shows that social mobility in Britain is high), politicians and the *intelligentsia* continue to imagine class barriers exist and hamper the latent powers of the British people. Even the last Conservative prime minister subscribed to this prejudice; when John Major accepted the leadership of his party, he famously declared:

This essay was originally published by the Centre for Policy Studies in *Policy Study* No. 154 (1997).
[1] *Financial Times,* 11 December 1975.

We aim for a classless society: not in the grey sense of drab uniformity—but in the sense that we remove the artificial barriers to choice and achievement.

And the politicians of the Left continue to blame the social ills of Britain on its "class structure." Even a supposed moderate such as Roy Hattersley still declares—from his seat in the House of Lords—that:

> There is not enough class war in Britain. . . . We keep hearing about the politics of envy but the British working classes are incredibly lacking in envy. They take what's coming to them, they accept their inferior position in society, they see other people enjoying privileges that they can never aspire to and they take it without a moment's resentment.[2]

Commentators such as Will Hutton also lay the blame for much of what has gone wrong in Britain at the door of the class system. In *The State We're In,* he admits:

> Throughout this book, the persistent theme has been the destructive role of "gentlemanly capitalism" and the privileged place occupied by finance and financial values in British society. Yet these do not appear out of a clear blue sky; they are socially produced, and the principal transmission mechanism is the British public school system.[3]

The underlying thrust is clear, namely, that the British class system is rigid and iniquitous and leaves large reservoirs of talent unused to the detriment of both social peace and economic efficiency. It is also alleged to be an instrument of exploitation. The allegations misconceive the character of British society and the nature of economic activity. They also ignore simple and undisputed facts of British history and of British social, economic, and political life. And the repetition of such false claims encourages a sense of passivity and disaffection among the nation's youth. As Professor Saunders has written in a recent analysis of social mobility in Britain:

> The game is worth playing, even for those born into the poorest social conditions. The mountain-tops are within reach. All that is needed is the ability and the will to start climbing.[4]

But if the poor are told that they will never be able to reach the top of the mountain, why should they ever start climbing?

---

[2] Quotation taken from the television programme, *Class,* broadcast on ITV on 10 June 1997.

[3] W. Hutton, *The State We're In* (New York: Vintage, 1996).

[4] P. Saunders, *Unequal but Fair? A Study of Class Barriers in Britain* (London: Institute of Economic Affairs, 1996).

STEREOTYPE AND REALITY

According to the stereotype, Britain is governed by a rich ruling caste. Yet Disraeli was prime minister from 1866 to 1868 and 1874 to 1880; Lloyd George, a very poor orphan brought up by an uncle who was a shoemaker, was chancellor of the exchequer by 1908 and prime minister from 1916 to 1922; and Ramsay MacDonald, illegitimate son of a fisherwoman, was prime minister in 1923–1924 and from 1929 to 1935. None of them had been to university; Lloyd George and MacDonald had elementary education only, and Disraeli attended a relatively unknown secondary school. More recently, although Mr. Heath and Mrs. Thatcher went to university, their backgrounds are not exactly upper class. Nor, of course, were those of Mr. Wilson, Mr. Callaghan, Mr. Healey, Mr. Kinnock, and Mr. Smith. Mr. Major, of course, came from a very modest background and left school at the age of sixteen with only two O-levels. Of the contenders for the leadership of the Conservative Party in 1997, Mr. Clarke, Mr. Hague, Mr. Howard, and Mr. Redwood all went to state schools and were, respectively, the sons of a watchmaker, a small businessman, a Romanian refugee, and a cost accountant.

Much critical comment on the role of class in British economic life is even more insubstantial. Those exposed to the stereotype could not guess that British industry is managed, and has been managed for decades or even centuries, by new men, people who have made their own way, often from humble beginnings. This is evident in the transport, food-processing, electronic, chemical, retailing, entertainment, building, property, and plantation industries. But it applies in a large measure also to steel, shipbuilding, and the mass circulation newspapers. The British motor industry has always been in the hands of new men or of American companies; therefore it would not be right to attribute its past troubles to class.

In the interwar period the leading figure of the British motor industry was Lord Nuffield, who began as a bicycle repairer and had had very little education. He made a large fortune, with part of which he founded Nuffield College. Indeed, it is quite usual to read accounts in the newspapers of the careers of very rich people who have started with nothing, side by side with articles complaining of the rigid class structure in Britain.

The richest man in Britain is, according to the *Sunday Times Rich List 1997*, Joseph Lewis. He was born in The Roman Arms, a pub in the East End of London where his father was landlord. His first fortune was made in catering; further fortunes were made in retailing, bureaux de change, and currency dealing. He is now one of the largest shareholders in the auction house, Christie's. At least twenty of the top one hundred richest people in the *Sunday Times* list are self-made. They include Jack Walker, the steel magnate; the Barclay twins, who started their professional life as decorators; Ann Gloag, a former nurse, who founded the bus company, Stagecoach with her brother Brian Souter; the musician Paul McCartney; the former Smithfields meat trader, David Thompson who founded the Hillsdown food and furniture group; Trevor Hemmings, a former apprentice bricklayer who now owns the largest stake in Center Parcs and Pontins; Bernie Eccleston, the man who owns and manages Formula One motor racing, has been the highest-paid Briton for the last three years. He is the son of a Suffolk trawlerman. Mark Dixon left school at sixteen to sell sandwiches; in 1988, at the age of twenty-eight, he set up Regus, which is today the largest provider of serviced offices in Europe; Sir John Hall, Paul Sykes, and Sir Graham Kirkham, all three the sons of miners, made their fortunes through, respectively, the Metro Centre development in Newcastle, the creation of the DFS furniture chain, and property development. Indeed, it is striking that there are six sons of coal miners in the list of the richest five hundred people in Britain. All in all, only 31 percent of the richest five hundred people in Britain inherited their wealth.

It has been just as possible for men from modest backgrounds to rise through to lead Britain's largest companies. Unilever, one of the most dynamic manufacturing companies in the world, grew out of a business started in the closing years of the nineteenth century by a Lancashire grocer who made his own soap. For many years the founder's successors as chairman and chief executive have been new men. Thus from 1960 to 1970 the position was held by Lord Cole, son of a clerk. Cole had a very modest education and started to work for the company at the age of seventeen. On retiring from Unilever, he became the government-appointed chairman of Rolls-Royce. (His son went to Eton and then to Oxford.) Its current chairman, Niall Fitzgerald, was born in Limerick and joined Unilever when he was twenty-two.

Less familiar are the names of Sir John Hay (1882–1964), undisputed leader of the British rubber industry of the interwar and early postwar years; Sir John Ellerman (1862–1933), founder of the Ellerman shipping line, who at the time of his death was possibly the richest man in England; the first Lord Catto (1879–1959), chairman of Yule Catto, director of Morgan Grenfell, and finally governor of the Bank of England. All three came from poor families and started their business careers in very modest jobs in city offices. David Robinson, who gave £17 million to found a Cambridge college in the 1970s, is also a self-made man.

The higher civil service and Oxford and Cambridge are often thought of as the exclusive preserve of the upper and upper-middle classes, at any rate before World War II. But the first Lord Stamp of Shortlands (1880–1940) began as a clerk in the Inland Revenue in 1896. He reached a high position before he retired young, moved into industry, became a director of the Bank of England and chairman of the largest British railway company. A more recent example of how humble birth is no barrier to advancement is the career of Sir Terence Burns. He is permanent secretary at HM Treasury and often referred to as the most powerful mandarin in Whitehall—yet he was born in a council house in the pit village of Hetton-le-Hole in Tyne and Wear.

At Oxford and Cambridge some of the highest and most coveted positions have always been held by new men of very modest background, including people who had not been undergraduates there. For instance, Sir James Chadwick, the famous physicist, was a Fellow of Gonville and Caius College, Cambridge, for most of the interwar period and became its Master in 1948. He was the son of an unskilled worker and went to Manchester University on a scholarship. The world of the arts and entertainment has also been open to men of talent: Sir Roy Strong was the son of a struggling commercial traveller but was appointed director of the National Portrait Gallery at the age of thirty-two and then director of the Victoria and Albert Museum when he was only thirty-nine. Similarly John Birt was born in Bootle into an extended family of Liverpool dockers—yet became director-general of the BBC by the age of forty-eight. And Melvyn Bragg, the TV presenter and director of London Weekend Television, was born and brought up in the family pub in Wigton, Cumberland.

Class domination of the British army before World War II is often thought to be so self-evident as not worth discussing. But for most of World War I the chief of the Imperial General Staff was Sir William Robertson (1860–1933). Robertson, who enlisted as a private in the 1880s, was the son of a landlady. He published his memoirs under the title *From Private to Field Marshal*. For most of his life he dropped his aitches.

Similarly, the Church of England has often been criticised as being dominated by the middle classes; yet George Carey, the present Archbishop of Canterbury, is the son of a hospital porter. He was born in the East End of London and left school at the age of fifteen.

Not even the diplomatic service was closed to people of humble origin. Sir Reader Bullard (1885–1976) was the son of an extremely poor casual labourer. He entered the consular service before World War I, having largely educated himself, and rose to become ambassador to Iran at a critical time.

Perhaps the greatest example of the heights to which men of talent can rise from beginnings however humble is the man who was the chancellor of Oxford University, president of the Royal Society of Literature, and leader of the Liberal Democrats in the Lords (he had also been Chancellor of the Exchequer, Home Secretary and President of the European Union). For Roy Jenkins, clubman, bon viveur, academic, historian, and politician was, despite appearances to the contrary, the son of a miner who went to prison in the Twenties for his part in the General Strike.

These are not isolated examples. They can be multiplied indefinitely. Prominent writers and scholars have recognised for well over a century the extensive social mobility in Britain and especially in British economic life. De Tocqueville commented on the ease of entry into the British aristocracy in the nineteenth century and the rise of new men in society and in business has often been noted at length by academics and others.

In 1959 Seymour Martin Lipset and Reinhard Bendix, two American sociologists, published an authoritative book, *Social Mobility in Industrial Society*,[5] in which they argued that the degree of social mobility, including that affecting business leadership, was much the same in Britain as in the United States. In that book they quote a study published in Britain in 1912 under the revealing title, *The Recruiting of the Employing Classes from the Ranks of the Wage Earners in the Cotton Industry*.[6] According to that study more than two-thirds of owners, directors, and managers in the cotton industry had begun their careers either as manual workers or in modest clerical positions. Lipset and Bendix wrote:

> The researchers, surprised by their own findings, attempted to check them by interviewing company executives, union leaders, and economic historians of the industry. They found general agreement with their findings. Sidney Webb, the Fabian leader, commented. "In Lancashire I think that practically all mill managers are taken from the ranks of the Spinners' Union."

But the findings are of interest on wider grounds. First, the British cotton industry at the time was a relatively old industry so that the large proportion of new men may be surprising. Second, the industry has contracted considerably since World War I, which suggests that Britain's industrial decline has nothing to do with the class system.

There are many other academic studies which show the high degree of social mobility in Britain. They are often by authors who are critical of British politics and society but who are nevertheless prepared to recognise evidence on this point. (Examples include books by Professors D. V. Glass and John Westergaard.)[7]

A major survey on social mobility was carried out in the late 1970s by a group of research workers under the direction of Dr John Goldthorpe, fellow of Nuffield College, Oxford. The results were noted in *New Society* of 10 November 1977 in an article which also emphasised the remarkable silence with which these highly interesting results were received. The article deserves to be quoted at some length:

[5] Lipset and Bendix, *Social Mobility* (Berkeley: University of California Press, 1959).

[6] S. J. Chapman and F. J. Marquis, *Journal of the Royal Statistical Society* 75 (1912): 293–306.

[7] D. V. Glass, *Social Mobility in Britain* (London: Routledge & Kegan Paul, 1954); J. Westergaard (with H. Resler), *Class in Capitalist Society* (London: Heinemann, 1975).

Over the past few months John Goldthorpe and his colleagues at Nuffield College, Oxford, have begun to publish the results of their analysis of social mobility in Britain in a variety of sociological journals. And these, for once, challenge rather than reinforce stereotypes. For they showed that Britain is a much more mobile society than the received wisdom suggests: that we are a surprisingly open society, with people moving up and down the occupational escalators in a bewilderingly complex pattern. For example, only a quarter of those in social class 1—managers and professionals—had fathers in the same category: rather less than the proportion drawn from a manual working-class background (at least partly, of course, because the managerial class has been expanding so fast that it simply couldn't recruit from among its own members).

Nor is the loud silence which has accompanied the publication of these findings an isolated example of the reaction to research which doesn't fit easily into conventional pigeon-holes.

The absurdities of trying to categorise people into a rigid class structure are well-illustrated by the following letter which appeared in the *Observer:*

> I was interested in your questionnaire on TV and had intended to complete it, until I noticed the usual horrid little box at the end, asking me to state my "class." According to the sociologists, I have two middle-class sisters and one working-class. I have one middle-class and one working-class daughter. My son-in-law was middle class until the age of twenty-three then became working class for three years. He is now middle class again. From now on I refuse to fill in any questionnaire which perpetuates such absurdity.[8]

Within the last eighteen months, two studies have been published which again provide notable confirmation of social mobility in Britain. In *Two Nations? The inheritance of poverty and affluence,*[9] Paul Johnson and Howard Reid examined the sons who ended up in the top fifth of income distribution and investigated where their fathers were in terms of income distribution. In a totally mobile society with no inheritance of aptitudes and no differentiation in education and upbringing, the sons in the top 20 percent would have fathers equally distributed across the entire income range, so that 20 percent of their fathers would have been in the top quintile down to 20 percent in the bottom quintile. The authors estimate that in fact 10 percent of the sons in the top quintile had fathers with incomes in the bottom quintile, compared with 34 percent of sons in the quintile whose fathers also had incomes in the top quintile. Whether or not this represents a *perfectly* mobile society, it surely proves that Britain is not the closed and blocked society imagined by some social critics.

[8] *The Observer,* 28 April 1976.

[9] P. Johnson and H. Reid, *Two Nations? The Inheritance of Poverty and Affluence* (London: Institute for Fiscal Studies, 1996).

In another recent paper,[10] Professor Saunders of Sussex University analysed data from the National Child Development Study (NCDS). This study traced the lives of a group of children since their birth in 1958 and investigates how they have fared during their school years and early careers. The parents of the individuals in the survey, and the individuals themselves, were grouped, by profession, into the classification system used by the Office of Population Censuses (OPCS). It showed that, dividing the classes into three groups (professionals; semi- and unskilled manual workers; and the "intermediate classes"), as many as 52 percent of the individuals studied had moved class. One-quarter of lower working class had been upwardly mobile into the middle class, and a further half had been upwardly mobile into the intermediate class.

In British economic life such mobility goes back many centuries. Professor Donald Macrae wrote:

> We have never, since Elizabethan times, had serious legal barriers to moving up or down social ladders, never had a closed nobility of the European kind. Our statistics, which on this matter take us back with some doubts to the early twentieth century, suggest a high and constant rate of mobility equal to that of the United States and greater than in Western Europe.[11]

His findings have not been disputed. Indeed, the expression "new rich" seems to have been used in England as early as the fifteenth century. And by the early eighteenth century Addison wrote:

> A superior capacity for business, and a more extensive knowledge, are steps by which a new man often mounts to favour, and out-shines the rest of his contemporaries.

Addison might almost have been anticipating the question asked by Lady Bracknell more than a century later in *The Importance of Being Earnest:* "Was he born in what the radical papers call the purple of commerce, or did he rise from the ranks of the aristocracy?"

THE RISE AND FALL OF BARRIERS

There have been few class barriers in access to wealth and to management in Britain. But after World War II, British economic society did become less open and less flexible than it had been in the past. It needed the reforms of Mrs. Thatcher's governments to reopen the road of opportunity.

In Britain the establishment and development of many businesses from small beginnings had become much more difficult by the 1970s. This was

---

[10] Saunders, *Unequal but Fair?*
[11] *The Daily Telegraph*, 19 November 1976.

the result of the nationalisation of many activities, widespread licensing, far-reaching bureaucratisation, and heavy taxation, both of persons and of small businesses. In addition, housing policy (primarily rent controls), trade union restrictions, minimum wages, so-called employment protection, and closed shops all reduced mobility both directly, and by making it more difficult to start new businesses, indirectly. These policies and measures made it difficult for people to rise from poverty to prosperity by means of legitimate business activity. For people of modest background such progress was largely restricted to those who could advance through the civil service or corporate bureaucracy or to the small number who could do so in the free professions. Many gifted working-class children (as well as many other people) had the capacity to establish and run small businesses, but neither the aptitudes or qualifications of a successful bureaucrat nor the skills required to succeed in a bureaucratic society.

The reforms of the last eighteen years removed many of these barriers: privatisation, the restraints imposed on the trade unions, deregulation, the sale of council houses, and the great reduction in income tax have all helped to create an environment in which talented people have been able to succeed.

The journalistic profession illustrates how the barriers had risen and fallen. From the early nineteenth century until the late 1970s, journalism presented an excellent opportunity of advance for talented people of working-class background and with little formal education. Some of the great figures of nineteenth-century and early twentieth–century British journalism, including outstanding and influential editors of *The Times* and *The Observer,* came from modest backgrounds and had little formal education. Compulsory unionisation and the widespread insistence on formal qualifications made such careers less likely in the late 1970s.

This closure of opportunities became well-recognised. An item in *The Times* referred to the careers of Louis Heren, deputy editor of *The Times,* and Admiral Sir Raymond Lygo, the vice-chief of Naval Staff.[12] They were messenger boys together on *The Times* and rose to their exalted positions from this beginning. The report concluded that in journalism such careers are not possible today. Again, Frank Johnson, then parliamentary sketch writer and editorial writer of the *Daily Telegraph* and now editor of the *Spectator,* received in January 1978 the award of Parliamentary Sketch Writer of the Year. He is the son of a working-class man, and his formal education terminated with one "O" level (in commerce). He started as a messenger boy on the *Sunday Express.* He is emphatic that, had the conditions of the 1970s endured, such a career would no longer be possible because of the widespread insistence on formal qualifications and career structure by unions and management. Today these restrictions have been

---

[12] *The Times,* 8 December 1977.

removed, and the media is once again a profession open to people from all backgrounds.

As a result of these numerous restrictions Britain was, by the 1970s, much less of an open society or economy—the sense of a society or economy with *carrière ouverte aux talents*—than it was formerly. The prospects of many talented working-class children had been prejudiced also by the abolition of many schools catering to their needs, and the replacement of these schools by institutions intended to serve as social engineering laboratories rather than as educational institutions. But these were not the complaints of the critics of the British class system.

These obstacles to social and economic mobility and advance owed much to the stereotype of the class system. The belief that British society is class-ridden and therefore restrictive paved the way for the politicisation and bureaucratisation of life. Measures introduced ostensibly to assist the poor and to promote greater equality and opportunity, in fact, restricted social, economic, and occupational mobility and made it more difficult for enterprising, ambitious, and self-reliant working-class people to get on. In the prevailing climate of opinion, these obstacles to movement had come to be attributed to a restrictive class system, an attribution which is then used spuriously to justify further extensions and the erection of further obstacles.

DIFFERENCES AND ADAPTABILITY

British society has for centuries displayed acute awareness of fine distinctions. The difference between a CB and a CBE is recognised to this day throughout the civil service, and often beyond it. Civil servants are unhappy to receive a CBE when they expect a CB, or an OBE when they hope for a CBE.

In matters such as education, speech, and dress, many freely and widely accepted distinctions are related to social standing and class. In this sense Britain has indeed always been a class society. But for about eight centuries Britain has not been a closed society, much less a caste society. Britain has not had a closed aristocracy or nobility since the early Middle Ages. Marriage, money, services, or official favour enabled many aspiring members of the working- and middle-classes to enter the aristocracy, including the highest ranks. Wolsey was the son of a Yorkshire butcher. Queen Elizabeth I was descended from a serf.

Nor could class barriers have obstructed economic progress or damaged the social fabric since no significant branch of British industry or commerce has ever been restricted to a particular class.

Until well into the nineteenth century Catholics, Jews, and Nonconformists could not enter politics or, for that matter, Oxford or Cambridge.

The practical effect of these restrictions on industry and commerce was extremely limited. Any significance was probably the exact opposite to what has often been suggested: these barriers induced ambitious people within these groups to go into industry and commerce. The restrictions may, therefore, have contributed to the conspicuous role of the Nonconformists in the development of British industry and commerce, notably so in such activities as banking, brewing, engineering, and textiles.

In the nineteenth and twentieth centuries the Nonconformists were joined by the Jews. Their economic success shows how misleading it is to think that exclusion from political activity necessarily inhibits the economic prospects of a person or a group. Jews had no political rights in Europe until well into the nineteenth century, by which time, however, many of them had become extremely rich and prominent in many forms of economic activity.

The presence and the unenforced acceptance of social distinctions and differences, including small differences and fine distinctions, was the outcome of centuries of relatively peaceful history. And, in an open and mobile society, such differences and distinctions do not restrict talent or inhibit economic progress. In fact, they rather promote ambition and achievement because they offer inducement, something to go for, at all levels of society.

The British upper classes usually absorb new men very easily. Indeed, the new recruits soon become indistinguishable from the class into which they have been recruited. The ease with which the upper classes absorb new men is apt to mislead casual observers and to lend surface plausibility to criticism. The situation, in fact, reflects the adaptability and tolerance of British society. But superficially it suggests a static society or even a rigid system. No one could have guessed the background of the late Sir James Chadwick from his conduct as master of Gonville and Caius College, Cambridge, which was founded in 1348, and of which he became master exactly six hundred years later. Much the same could be said about Sir John Hay and about Lord Cole, whom I have already mentioned.

After only a single generation, persons of working-class origin can merge completely into the aristocracy. Thus the career, connections, and even the physical appearance of the late Lord Robertson of Oakridge (1896–1974) would have suggested that he was an aristocrat. He was a general, British High Commissioner, Commander-in-Chief in the Middle East, ADC to two monarchs, company director and chairman of the British Transport Commission. He was the son of Field Marshal Sir William Robertson, a plebeian in appearance and some of his manners. Again, when Granada recently announced its plans for a hostile take-over of the Forte group, much was made of the fact that the Chairman of Granada, Gerry Robinson was one of nine children of an Irish carpenter. Yet Rocco Forte's father had arrived in England a poor man and started the Forte empire with one milk bar in Regent Street.

The conjunction of assumed rigidity and actual flexibility of the social system sets up pitfalls which can trap the unwary. When Sir Sydney Caine became the director of the London School of Economics, one newspaper said that he had been educated at Harrow; in fact he had attended Harrow County School, a very different establishment.

CLASS, EXPLOITATION, AND EDUCATION

Some variants of the principal line of criticism of the British class system deserve notice. One of these is the suggestion, sometimes explicit, sometimes implied, that the prosperity of the well-to-do has been extracted from the rest of the population. There have always been some groups or individuals who have benefited from monopoly, or from state subsidies, or from political manipulation. But even in the aggregate, such instances have not been of major overall significance in the industrial and commercial fortunes over the last two hundred years.

The allegedly restrictive character and class bias of English education is often blamed for various economic and social difficulties. However, the educational system did not preclude rapid British economic progress in the eighteenth and nineteenth centuries, promoted and propelled largely by people with little formal education, a phenomenon which academics and educationalists seem reluctant to recognise. Moreover, neither the presence nor the privileges of Oxford and Cambridge, nor the prestige of the public schools enabled them to stop other groups from setting up academies and schools. There was no general state education in England until well into the nineteenth century, but there was no official barrier to the setting up of educational institutions. Again, the educational system in Scotland was quite different from that in England. There were old universities in Scotland, and these were not restricted to members of the Church of England, nor controlled by it, and the school system there was also more extensive than in England. Yet Scotland has not outdistanced England either in economic performance or in industrial relations. Nor is it sensible to describe the restrictions of the educational system as class-bound, when those against whom it discriminated included aristocrats such as the Catholic Dukes of Norfolk.

Much has been made of the large proportion of prime ministers and cabinet ministers in the twentieth century who had been to Oxford and Cambridge. This is not evidence of the allegedly closed character of British politics. To a considerable extent it reflects the prestige which ability and education commanded in British politics until recently; the inclination of those with political ambition to go to university, coupled with the emphasis at Oxford and Cambridge on studies helpful in political life; and the access of gifted persons from all ranks of society to these universities. The careers of Mr. Wilson, Mr. Heath, Mrs. Thatcher, Mr. Healey, and all of the recent contenders for the leadership of the Conservative party reflect the open nature of Oxford and Cambridge rather than the allegedly closed character of British political life.

POISE AND VULNERABILITY

The relatively peaceful history of Britain, the absence of foreign invasion or occupation and of violent revolutions (at any rate since the mid-seventeenth century), and the ready acceptance of differences, including social differences, imparted poise and self-assurance to the upper and upper-middle classes and to the representatives of traditional institutions. This poise made it possible to resist outside pressures. A Cambridge college, an institution widely regarded as class—highly ridden and insular, has unhesitatingly elected foreigners to—coveted fellowships at times of substantial unemployment or at times when the country was swept by xenophobia. Similarly, it was able to elect to a fellowship a scholar from Communist China a few days after a Chinese force heavily defeated a British regiment in Korea. Such action is far less likely, perhaps even unthinkable, in American and Continental universities, which are generally thought to be much less class-ridden and restrictive than Oxford and Cambridge.

But the prolonged and largely unquestioned acceptance of differences and distinctions also made for vulnerability, in that the upper and upper-middle classes were not forced to examine or rationalise their position. They were thus ill-placed to face the upsurge of egalitarianism in the Western world. Having taken their situation for granted, they could not analyse or explain it. Their spokesmen or representatives knew and, perhaps, could even articulate the distinction in rank between a baron, a baronet, and a knight, or even between a CB and a CBE, but not that between a differentiated yet open and mobile society on the one hand and a restrictive, closed, or caste society on the other. Nor were they able to scrutinise effectively such arguments as that the incomes of the well-to-do had been secured at the expense of the poor. They were thus unable to counter the arguments such as those often adduced for egalitarian policies or in favour of the far-reaching privileges to trade unions. More generally, they were unable to resist effectively the arguments and sentiments which resulted in the politicisation of social and economic life, a politicisation often deemed necessary to offset the alleged restrictive class bias in British politics.

The upper and middle classes were intellectually unarmed to meet the egalitarian thrust, perhaps even more than are businessmen to meet the more specifically economic arguments of self-styled egalitarians. The resulting loss of poise and nerve was accentuated by the emergence of a guilt feeling over the presence of differences, in the face of growing belief that all such differences are abnormal and reprehensible.

INTELLECTUALS AND EGALITARIANS

British intellectuals are much more preoccupied with class than their counterparts on the Continent, where class distinctions have usually been much clearer and firmer. There may be various reasons for this preoccupation of British intellectuals. Because they read and write English, they are apt to compare British society with American society (which on the surface at any rate is more open than British society), rather than with the other societies which in any case they know much less well. The long and relatively peaceful continuity of British history and society may have been a more important factor.

The absence of violent change has suggested a stable social system and an impregnable and static ruling class. The unobtrusive ease with which new men rose in the social scale and became indistinguishable from their former social superiors reinforces the plausibility of this suggestion. The open and mobile character of British society compared to continental society may also have enhanced preoccupation with class. It made the aristocracy and the prosperous groups more accessible and conspicuous and thus more envied and resented than elsewhere. They became more obvious targets than their counterparts abroad.

The reasons which I have suggested for the obsession of the British intelligentsia with class are conjectural. But whatever the reasons behind the misleading stereotype of the class system, its widespread acceptance has sustained policies which are restrictive, which obstruct economic achievement and advance, and which cause resentment and even bitterness. As I have noted earlier, these sentiments are misdirected because they are based on mistaken ideas about the forces behind the restrictive measures.

The persistent harping on differences and distinctions is not designed to bring about equality, but to promote a thoroughly politicised society in which all aspects of life are subject to political direction. But the large-scale, politically enforced reduction of social and economic differences, serves only to exacerbate another difference, namely that between rulers and subjects. Those who do not relish this prospect will do well to examine critically the stereotype of the class system and also ponder both the background of social and economic differences and the ultimate objective of ostensibly egalitarian measures.

XII

Egalitarianism: A Delicate Dilemma

I

The wide economic differences between people in an open and free society result from differences in aptitudes, motivations, and circumstances. State action to remove these economic differences entails such extensive coercion that the society ceases to be open and free. Here lies the central dilemma for egalitarians. The implications of the dilemma and of the persistent, widespread failure to recognize them form the central argument of this essay.

II

A discrepancy between an assumed norm or expectation and social reality is commonly described as a "social problem." Inasmuch as social scientists are largely preoccupied with discerning, announcing, and emphasizing discrepancies between norms or expectations and reality, they tend to generate social problems rather than solve them. An example is the extensive concern with economic differences. Indeed, in recent years there has been an upsurge of interest in this subject, on the international level as well as the domestic.

The appeal of egalitarianism is likely to persist. In recent decades incomes have risen greatly in the West, and income differences have narrowed. But as de Tocqueville observed, when social differences have narrowed, those which remain appear especially irksome and objectionable; and, as he also pointed out, material advance is apt to engender discontent over failure to have achieved more or to have achieved some other objective.

The contemporary predilection for numbers and quantification, together with the emphasis on material conditions, have helped further to focus attention on economic differences. Even when reliable and free from conceptual problems, which is unusual, statistics of income, income differences, and changes in such data tell us little or nothing about the background of

This is an extended version of the paper first published in *The Times Literary Supplement* (London), 23 July 1976; it is reprinted here with permission of the *Supplement*. Subsequently this essay was reprinted by the International Institute for Economic Research as Reprint Paper 4, January 1997.

the situation, including the process by which the condition has emerged. Yet, how a social situation has arisen is usually basic for worthwhile assessment. Incomes can become more equal as a result of such radically different changes as a relative decline in the birthrate of the poor, or relative increase in their mortality, or expropriation of the rich, or an increase in capital relative to unskilled labor, or technical change, or still other reasons. Conventional statistics by themselves tell us nothing about these radical differences and their causes.

III

Once the moral and political case for egalitarian policies is taken for granted, the movement for more and more egalitarianism perpetuates itself. If the results of egalitarian policies are deemed satisfactory, it is often presumed that still more can be achieved by more extensive efforts; if, on the other hand, the policies are deemed to have failed, it is generally concluded that they were not drastic enough. Such reactions are predictable when the economic positions of different individuals and groups are thought to depend largely on public policy—as, indeed, they often are when economic life is heavily politicized (partly the result of egalitarianism itself).

Exercise of state authority implies inequality of power between ruler and subjects. Political power implies the ability of rulers forcibly to restrict the choices open to those they rule. Enforced reduction or removal of economic differences emerging from voluntary arrangements extends and intensifies the inequality of coercive power. The wider the differences in the circumstances and in the aptitudes and ambitions of those whose economic well-being is to be (at least partially) equalized, the greater the intensity, extent, and duration of the coercion required for the purpose—and thus the more pronounced becomes the inequality of power.

Possession of wealth and the presence of economic differences do not imply ability of the wealthy to restrict the choices open to others and thus to coerce them. In a modern open society, the accumulation of wealth, especially great wealth, normally results from activities which extend the choices of others—as illustrated by the fortunes acquired in mass retailing or in development of the automobile. The absence of coercive power in most forms of successful economic activity is recognized in Dr. Johnson's familiar observation that "there are few ways in which a man can be more innocently employed than in getting money."

Differences in readiness to utilize economic opportunities—willingness to innovate, to assume risk, to organize—are highly significant in explaining economic differences in open societies. This is evident. The opportunities seized by a few were available to many. This has always been the case throughout the West—and, indeed, elsewhere, as shown by the many Chinese *nouveaux riches* in the East. Income differences resulting from readiness to benefit from economic opportunities will be especially wide when there is rapid social, economic, and technical change, including the development of new products and the opening of new markets.

Purported belief in the basic equality of people's economic faculties and ambitions has enabled egalitarians to ignore the main dilemma of egalitarian ideology. It has also colored terminology. If people are assumed to be equally endowed and motivated and yet there are wide economic differences, it would seem that some undefined but malevolent force has perverted the course of events. This discrepancy between assumption and reality may account for the habitual references to economic "inequality" rather than to economic "differences." (The latter term is more appropriate, not implicitly prejudging the issue.)

The same discrepancy between implication and actuality may explain also the familiar but anomalous interpretation of social justice as meaning substantially equal incomes. This interpretation is anomalous because it is not obviously just to penalize those who have contributed more to the social product for the benefit of others who have contributed less—unless it is assumed that incomes are not earned but extracted.

It is widely believed, or at least often asserted, that relatively high incomes are somehow extracted rather than earned, that is, produced. Incomes of certain groups are indeed sometimes increased by monopoly power or, more commonly, by state action. But the idea is misconceived that incomes of the relatively prosperous are secured generally at the expense of the rest of the community.

This misconception has often had lamentable consequences. It has encouraged the maltreatment and even destruction of economically productive groups, including ethnic and religious minorities. (The fate of such prosperous groups at the hands of political masters illustrates the inadequacy of wealth by itself to confer power or even ensure survival. Indeed, the possession of wealth often results in political vulnerability.) The same misconception colors familiar references to "shares," usually unequal shares, of different groups in the national product and lies behind assertions that certain groups have not shared adequately in national or world prosperity—assertions which ignore the question of how little these groups may have contributed to the prosperity.

The unfortunate terminology of egalitarian discourse and, to some extent, of the economic theory of distribution may have contributed to the misconception. As already noted, inequality is an infelicitous term. The same is true of the expression, "distribution of income," which suggests that there is a preexisting income which somehow gets divided. But incomes normally are earned, produced by their recipients, not "distributed" to them.

"Redistribution" also is misleading because it is not a preexisting income which is being reallocated. Rather, parts of resources are taken from those who produced them and handed to others, whose incomes are thereby augmented beyond what they have produced.

IV

It is often assumed that income differences will be readily accepted when they plainly reflect achievement. The contrary is just as likely. Lack of economic success is apt to be keenly felt and resented when economic achievement is emphasized and when failure is imputed to inadequacy. When faced with economic success in an open society, many deny that the success reflects even a contribution to society, much less merit.

Equality of opportunity was until recently the principal thrust of egalitarian ideology. For example, many Fabians, notably R. H. Tawney, thought that equality of opportunity would result in substantial equality of incomes; any remaining income differences would reflect merit and would, therefore, be widely respected and readily accepted. Such ideas bypass the intractable problems behind the central dilemma of egalitarianism: granted that equals should be treated equally, how shall we treat those who are unequally endowed, motivated, or situated?

"Equality of opportunity" is elusive and imprecise. Certain cultures emphasize education and economic productivity and, predictably, confer material advantages on their members—advantages which do not always conduce happiness, dignity, or sensitivity. Some people are advantaged by loving parents or a cultivated background. Good looks and attractive personality result in unequal opportunities. Attempts to offset such advantages, say by taxation, conflict with other criteria of equality—including the principle that equal incomes should bear equal taxes.

An open society—that is, one with *la carrière ouverte aux talents*—is the most familiar interpretation of the ambiguous concept of equality of opportunity. But the open society is obviously incompatible with substantial equality of income and wealth because of the wide personal and group differences in economic aptitudes and motivations. These differences are evident in the rise from poverty to prosperity of countless individuals and groups the world over; in the wide differences in prosperity between religious and ethnic groups in different areas and societies for centuries; and in the material success of certain communities in the face of adverse official discrimination—for example, nonconformists, Huguenots, and Jews in the West, and the Chinese communities in Southeast Asia.

It is only the naive belief that everyone's aptitudes and motivations are the same—a belief sinister in its consequences—which supports the notion that an open society is practically synonymous with economic equality or virtually ensures it. It is extraordinary that this should have been believed for so long when the evidence to the contrary is both overwhelming and obvious.

The belief in uniform economic aptitudes and motivations is a facet of the doctrine of the natural equality of man, the idea that all of us are the same except for accidental or nefariously imposed differences in wealth and education. The poor are like the rich minus the money. The peoples of the Third World are all much of a muchness and differ from those of the West only in having less money.

V

The principal cost of egalitarian policies is usually thought to be reduction of efficiency and hence of material progress. This cost, which certainly is real and considerable, is expressed in such formulations as the trade-off between equality (often identified with equity) and efficiency. Such formulations recognize that economic activity is not a zero-sum game but a process of production of goods and services, the flow of which is affected by attitudes and policies.

Although the economic cost of egalitarianism is real and its ramifications are manifold, I shall not discuss it in this article. The dilemma I emphasize here lies in the surrender of freedom for the promised reduction or removal of economic differences.

If people's circumstances and capacities, including economic aptitudes and motivations, were substantially the same, incomes would be largely equal in an open society. Thus the establishment of such a society would suffice for economic equality, without special taxation, let alone more drastic interference with voluntary arrangements. In fact, differences in circumstances, motivations, and aptitudes, including the ability to seize economic opportunities, ensure appreciable differences in incomes in an open society. Political action to reduce these differences or prevent their emergence requires an extension of state power incompatible with a free society.

As wide income differences have not disappeared in open societies, so pressures for their reduction or even elimination also have continued. Hence the demands for increasing the scope and level of what is misleadingly termed redistributive taxation. It is misleading because, as noted, it is not a preexisting income that is being redistributed. Rather, part of the incomes of producers is confiscated for the benefit of others, including those who derive political or personal advantage from advocating or administering the confiscation.

The imposition of specific disabilities, in addition to progressive taxation, on individuals and groups with cultural and personal characteristics conducive to economic success is now widely advocated and to a considerable extent practiced. Special taxation of talented persons has been proposed on the argument that their talents should be regarded as communal property. Such proposals mean conscription of abilities, which is to some extent implicit also in progressive taxation. The removal of children from their parents and even manipulation of the genetic code also have been suggested as instruments for the promotion of equality, although thus far generally dismissed. Quotas handicapping the ambitious and the gifted have already been widely adopted in higher education and in certain areas of economic activity in the United States.

In an open society, attempts to eliminate, or even substantially to reduce, income differences extend coercive power, that is, inequality of power between rulers and ruled. This also implies politicization of economic life, a situation in which economic activity depends largely on political decisions, and in which the incomes of people and their economic *modus vivendi* are prescribed principally by politicians and bureaucrats. How far-reaching is the required coercion and politicization of economic life will depend on the degree of economic equality the rulers intend to achieve; they will depend also on the various aptitudes, motivations, and circumstances of the groups and individuals among whom economic differences are to be reduced.

Extensive politicization of life enhances the prizes of political power and thus the stakes in the fight for them. This in turn exacerbates political tension, at least until opposition is forcibly suppressed or effectively demoralized. And because people's economic fortunes come to depend so largely on political and administrative decisions, the attention, energies, and resources of forward-looking, perceptive, and ambitious people are diverted from economic activity to political machination.

These consequences are manifest in many societies, especially in multiracial communities. Politicization of life, often pursued in the name of equality, has in many countries brought about a situation in which the question of who controls the government has become a matter of overriding importance, even a matter of life and death to millions. The effect of this on people's fears, feelings, and conduct is observable in numerous countries where there is ethnic diversity, including the United Kingdom. It stands out starkly in the profoundly heterogeneous societies of the Third World. The ferocity of political struggle in many Third World countries cannot be understood without an awareness of the politicization of life there—a process helped along by slogans of equality and intensified by the idea that incomes are extracted, not earned.

VI

Differences in income and wealth reflect to a large extent aptitudes and motivations, not only in open societies but also to a considerable degree in societies which are not open, but not completely closed or caste. The poor usually comprise a disproportionate number of people who lack the capabilities and inclinations for distinctive economic achievement, and often for cultural achievement as well. Most agree that weak members of a society should be helped. But why people are poor is fundamental for sensible remedial action.

Those who are poor as a result of crippling disease, or unavoidable or uninsurable accident, or erosion of savings through inflation may be thought to deserve and require treatment different from that directed to those who simply and habitually overspend their incomes. Large-scale penalization of productive groups for the benefit of the materially and culturally less productive—and for the benefit also of those who administer wealth transfers—impairs the prospects of a society. Pronounced adverse effects are especially probable when the support of the less productive is given without stigma and as of right—even more so when those who are more productive are made to feel guilty. These are precisely the stances and attitudes prominent in the advocacy and practice of redistribution.

Support without stigma, as of right, is reflected in the terminology of the "negative income tax." The payment of tax on produced income is a statutory obligation. Conversely, the receipt of a negative income tax is now deemed a right to an income regardless of performance, simply by virtue of being alive and relatively poor. It should be added that personal and group differences in economic aptitudes and motivations are likely to frustrate expectations that guarantee of a cash income would make it possible to abolish specific welfare services. These services will still have to be supplied to the many recipients of cash payments who will fail to provide for the contingencies of life. Such people are likely to be disproportionately numerous among the poorest, that is, the recipients of negative income tax. In Britain this is suggested by the prevalence of avoidable ill health and dental decay among children of unskilled workers who own television sets.

Support without stigma is conspicuous in the administration of international wealth transfers. Third World governments receiving foreign aid are habitually termed "partners in progress," when in fact they are recipients of doles or alms. And even more often than in domestic wealth transfers, these donations (often misleadingly termed "development finance") are advocated as restitution for past wrongs. Many recipients of both domestic and international wealth transfers are paupers, in the traditional sense of persons dependent on officially provided largesse. But because the support is given as of right and even envisaged as compensation for historical sins, the paupers can not only insist on being given these transfers, but can even prescribe the political conduct of the donors. This is the case on the domestic scene, and it is much more evident on the global scene.

VII

The promotion of economic equality and the reduction of poverty are objectives which are separate and may conflict. Egalitarian measures often benefit middle-income groups at the expense both of the rich and of the poor. They also commonly obstruct social and economic mobility, discourage the accumulation and effective deployment of capital, and inhibit enterprise. They thereby damage the interests of the poor as well as the wealthy.

Greater equality of income and relief of poverty share the characteristic that contemporary debate about their attainment is pervaded by determinism. The poor are often envisaged as a distinct class at the mercy of the environment, with no will of their own, while at the same time they are denied the primary human characteristic of responsibility. The rich are regarded as having a will of their own, but as being villainous. Poverty is seen as a *condition* caused by external forces, while prosperity, is viewed as the result of *conduct*, although reprehensible conduct. The poor are considered passive but virtuous, the rich as active but wicked. Bureaucrats and social reformers—and at times also academics, artists, media sorts, and entertainers—are distinct categories who seem to get the best of both worlds: they may be prosperous and yet retain virtue.

VIII

Egalitarian policies which are often entwined with these unfounded attitudes towards the poor and the rich are also commonly rooted in other chimeric concepts, for example, general theories of history. From this perspective, the extension of state power entailed in egalitarian policies is sometimes felt to be justified by an assumption of successive stages in the course of history, stages which are considered inevitable and ought not to be delayed. This particular underpinning of egalitarian policies along with its hallmark methodology warrants our attention.

Anyone presenting a theory of history is confronted by countless events and sequences from which he perforce must choose. Supporters of a particular theory can always find events and interpretations in support of that theory. They can do so whether they think their generalizations (the uniformity's they claim to have discerned), that is, the so-called laws of history, reflect the unfolding of God's will or the influence of economic determinism. That way lies arbitrariness, both in the choice of events and in their interpretation. These considerations apply generally to theories of history and also to attempts to divide its course into specific stages. Successful division of a sequence into distinct stages requires that the stages themselves, the turning points and the processes by which one stage leads to another, are distinct and definable. The life cycles of living organisms satisfy these criteria. So-called stages of history generally do not.

Furthermore, social scientists and some historians, especially Marxist historians, often personify collectivities, such as city-states or underdeveloped countries, and endow them with powers to make decisions, express sentiments, and pursue courses of action. This familiar practice obscures the fact that these decisions are taken by persons either individually or in groups, who face choices, and who *ex ante* have to weigh costs, risks, and results. They normally do not know what the outcome will be, and observers cannot normally predict their decisions.

Most historical events and sequences do not issue in unique and unambiguous results. Widely different results can emerge from given initial conditions. Close inquiry of the *ex post* situation is necessary to find out which of several and often numerous possible results have actually issued from a particular antecedent situation. And even the definition or interpretation of the initial conditions, as well as the assessment of large and apparently obvious facts, requires more than a casual glance over one's shoulder. To speculate about situations and processes without looking at actual experience is to risk losing touch with reality.

Neither statistical inference nor the examination of the implications of situations can serve as a basis for a theory of history. This is the reason for the inadequacy of economic determinism as the explanation of world economic history. The explanation and predictions of the course of history derived from economic determinism have been spectacularly unsuccessful, without affecting its appeal. Nor has this appeal been diminished by frequent exposure of its shortcomings, such as its evident irrelevance to major decisions which have shaped historical events; or the many obvious instances when people have taken decisions contrary to their material interests. Indeed, economic determinism has often led its exponents to diametrically opposite inferences from what they thought passed as analysis of a particular situation. In the 1930s some adherents of economic determinism argued that capitalism must necessarily lead to war, on the ground that only large-scale production of arms or even outright war can prevent the collapse of the capitalist system. Other economic determinists insisted that capitalism must lead to appeasement or even to total surrender by the West, became the capitalists could not tolerate the disruption of the profit system.

Construction of a general theory of history to cover all ages and all mankind is a will-o'-the-wisp.[1] The attempt is both sterile and damaging. It generally diverts attention and effort from more modest but much more informative and intellectually rewarding endeavors. Such endeavours may well appear pedestrian beside the attempts to construct a general theory of history, but they are likely to tell us far more about reality, either past or present. The quest for a general theory of history can also have more widely damaging results. Many of those who have claimed to have discerned the laws of history have simultaneously claimed it as their right, or even as their duty, to interpret and to enforce these laws. They have claimed it as their mission to bring about and hasten an outcome which was in any case inevitable. The pretense of having successfully discovered such laws has served as spurious moral or intellectual justification for such conduct. For instance, it has served to underpin the Marxist-Leninist position at popular, academic, and political levels, and it continues to underlie egalitarian policies.

REFERENCES

Original Papers

Allen, Francis A. *The Criminal Law as an Instrument of Economic Regulation*. June 1976.

Cogan, John, M. Bruce Johnson, and Michael P. Ward. Introduction by Hendrik S. Houthakker. *Energy and Jobs: A Long Run Analysis*. August 1976.

Friedman, Milton. Introduction by Joseph J. Spengler. *Adam Smith's Relevance for 1976*. December 1976.

McCracken, Paul W. *Reflections on Economic Advising: A Paper and an Interview*. March 1976.

Meltzer, Allan H. Introduction by Roger A. Freeman. *Why Government Grows*. August 1976.

Reprint Papers

Allen, Francis A. Introduction by R. H. Coase. *The Causes of Popular Dissatisfaction With Legal Education*. January 1977.

Hoag, Malcolm W. *United States Foreign Policy: Why Not Project Interdependence by Design?* October 1976.

Kristol, Irving, and Peter T. Bauer. Introduction by Cotton M. Lindsay. *Two Essays on Income Distribution and the Open Society*. January 1977.

Walters, Alan A. Introduction by Harry G. Johnson. *The Politicization of Economic Decisions*. April 1976.

[1] See Peter Bauer, "Economic History as Theory," in *The Development Frontier* (London: Harvester Wheatsheaf, 1991), p. 166.

NEW FORUM BOOKS

New Forum Books makes available to general readers outstanding original interdisciplinary scholarship with a special focus on the juncture of culture, law, and politics. New Forum Books is guided by the conviction that law and politics not only reflect culture but help to shape it. Authors include leading political scientists, sociologists, legal scholars, philosophers, theologians, historians, and economists writing for nonspecialist readers and scholars across a range of fields. Looking at questions such as political equality, the concept of rights, the problem of virtue in liberal politics, crime and punishment, population, poverty, economic development, and the international legal and political order, New Forum Books seeks to explain—not explain away—the difficult issues we face today.

Paul Edward Gottfried, *After Liberalism: Mass Democracy in the Managerial State*

Peter Berkowitz, *Virtue and the Making of Modern Liberalism*

John E. Coons and Patrick M. Brennan, *By Nature Equal: The Anatomy of a Western Insight*

David Novak, *Covenantal Rights: A Study in Jewish Political Theory*

Charles L. Glenn, *The Ambiguous Embrace: Government and Faith-Based Schools and Social Agencies*

Peter Bauer, From Subsistence to Exchange *and Other Essays*

Robert P. George, ed., *Great Cases in Constitutional Law*